THE DANCE

THE DANCE

AN HISTORICAL SURVEY OF DANCING IN EUROPE

BY

CECIL J. SHARP

Founder of The English Folk Dance Society

AND

A. P. OPPÉ

With a New Introduction
by
Richard Rastall, M.A., MUS.B., PH.D.

ROWMAN AND LITTLEFIELD
TOTOWA, NEW JERSEY

THIS REPRINT EDITION FIRST PUBLISHED IN
THE UNITED STATES 1972
by Rowman and Littlefield, Totowa, New Jersey

Bibliographic Note

The Frontispiece and Plates 1, 2 and 3, which were in colour in the 1924
edition, are reproduced in monochrome in this reprint.

ISBN 0 87471 105 3

First Published 1924

by Halton & Truscott Smith Ltd., London
and Minton, Balch & Company, New York

This edition published by kind
permission of the copyright holder

25-7248

Printed in Great Britain by
Scolar Press Limited, Menston, Yorkshire

INTRODUCTION

by Richard Rastall, M.A., MUS.B., PH.D.
University of Leeds

Cecil J. Sharp (1859-1924) is best remembered for his work on English folk song, a body of research that had obvious repercussions on English music earlier this century. In 1903 he noted down his first folk song, 'The Seeds of Love', at Hambridge in Somerset; only four years later he published *English Folk-Song: Some Conclusions*, the work on which rests his main reputation as a pioneer. During those years Sharp started the publication of *Folk-Songs from Somerset* (1904-09), the first of his collections of folk songs, and he also contributed to the *Journal* of the Folk-Song Society.

Sharp believed that folk song was in danger of extinction, and the greater part of his published work consists of collections of folk songs with his own piano accompaniments added. He soon realised, however, that the songs were not the only folk music threatened, and he turned to the related subject of folk dance. His attention had been drawn to the dance quite by accident, and it is even a little surprising that a professional musician should have become so involved in one of the mimetic arts. Sharp saw his first folk dance in 1899. On Boxing Day that year, walking in Headington, near Oxford, he witnessed the performance of a Morris: he noted the tune down, but was unable to make any record of the dancers' movements. Clearly, if the dance (as opposed to its music) was to be recorded, it was necessary to find or evolve a notation for the arm- and leg-movements.

From about 1906 onwards Sharp turned his attention to the dance, investigating the sword dances of northern England, the Morris dances of the Midlands and the English Country Dance, all with the same thoroughness with which he had collected folk songs. The results of this work were three large collections of dances, together with companion collections of tunes—*The Morris Book* and *Morris Dance Tunes* (1907-13), *The Country Dance Book* and *Country Dance Tunes* (1909-22), and *The Sword Dances of Northern England* and *The Sword Dances of Northern England—Song and Dance Airs* (1911-13). In the light of his experience, especially of the Country Dance, Sharp also studied Playford's *The English Dancing Master* (1651 and later editions): his work on this source constituted a major advance in the historical and social study of the dance, and—most important of all, perhaps—his elucidation of Playford's directions (which has not yet been bettered) made it possible to revive the dances and to perform them correctly.

This work involved what should probably be regarded as the instrument of Sharp's finest achievement for the folk-song movement: he devised a system of verbal and diagrammatic notation (described as 'masterly' by Margaret Dean Smith*) by means of which dances could be transmitted. One can—and should—question Sharp's definition of 'folk' as opposed to 'popular' music, with the consequent inconsistencies in the repertory collected; and one needs to watch for those passages in his writings where speculation is offered as if it were historical fact. But his work in preserving the traditional dances of this country is another matter. If there were nothing else to thank him for (and there is a great deal) Sharp would be gratefully remembered for this.

Sharp's enthusiasm attracted kindred spirits, and in 1911 he founded the English Folk Dance Society. For the next three years the Society was the base for much team-work in the collecting of traditional dances: but the team-work was largely broken up in 1914, when many of Sharp's younger colleagues went to fight in the war. Sharp continued to work on his dance collections, for although his visit to America in the latter part of the war resulted in a concentrated spell of research on song, culminating in the publication in 1917 of *English Folk Songs from the Appalachian Mountains*, publication of *The Country Dance Book* and *Country Dance Tunes* was completed only in 1922. The following year he started work on two projects, both of which were left incomplete at his death in 1924: one was a translation and interpretation of Arbeau's *Orchésographie*, the other an historical survey of the dance, published soon after his death and here reprinted.

The Dance—An Historical Survey of Dancing in Europe is clearly not quite the book that Sharp envisaged: given another year of life he would almost certainly have expanded certain sections of the book, and would have made the type of modification suggested by Oppé (pp. xii-xiii). Equally clearly, the book's value to the student of the dance is incalculable: the text has never been superseded as a general survey, even though certain areas covered by it have since been worked in more detail—for example, in Mabel Dolmetsch's *Dances of England and France from 1450 to 1600* (London, 1949)—while the illustrations constitute in themselves an historical survey that is far more than a mere commentary on, or elucidation of, the text.

The text is based both on the various treatises on dancing and on Sharp's own unrivalled knowledge of traditional dances. It is therefore one of the first works to use consistently the principle that comparative study of an art in the present day can throw light on the history of the art. This principle has since been used by musicologists in certain fields for which written evidence is non-existent or unsatisfactory: for instance, the study of medieval and Renaissance dance-music is made easier by the fact that many of the contemporary instruments survive in certain

* John Playford, *The English Dancing Master* (*1651*): facsimile reprint, with an Introduction, Bibliography and Notes by Margaret Dean-Smith (London, 1957), p. xix.

countries as folk instruments. Sharp's proposition concerning the dance (page 3) is an explanation of precisely this principle: '... the racial or folk-dance still survives in various forms in the several nations of Europe, and its .... characteristics can be observed and noted'.

It is a great loss to posterity that Sharp was not able to study in detail the dances from more of the 'several nations of Europe'. Nevertheless, *The Dance*, his last published work and the summary of his research on the subject, stands as a fitting monument to his scholarship and energy.

MARCH 1972

THE DANCE

P. L. DEBUCOURT. LE MENUET DE LA MARIÉE. 1786 AQUATINT IN COLOURS.

THE DANCE

AN HISTORICAL SURVEY OF DANCING IN EUROPE

BY

CECIL J. SHARP

Founder of The English Folk Dance Society

AND

A. P. OPPÉ

1924

London: Halton & Truscott Smith, Ltd.

New York: Minton, Balch & Company.

(Printed in Great Britain)

CONTENTS.

LIST OF ILLUSTRATIONS.

viii.

ix.

ILLUSTRATIONS IN TEXT.

PREFACE.

During his absence from England for reasons of health in the winter of 1923, Cecil Sharp threw himself with his customary keenness into the study of Thoinot-Arbeau's *Orchésographie*, and he found that the experience gained in interpreting Playford's *Dancing-Master* and devising a system of notation for the English Dances which he himself revived, enabled him to solve several points of difficulty in the text of the earliest of choreographers which had baffled previous historians. On his return to London his interest in this study and in the early dances generally, coupled with his delight in the latest dance picture which I had found for him—it was the print by Martinet of the *Danse du Mai* at Versailles in 1763, of which we have been able to reproduce the original drawing through the kindness of its owner, the Honourable Irwin Laughlin, of Washington—suggested that we might together bring out a volume on the History of Dancing, in which both text and illustrations should be based on contemporary sources such as those which he was studying. There was the immediate advantage in a work of this kind that it would amuse and occupy him while he was confined to the house by the doctor's orders. Further, we hoped that if the experiment proved successful it would lead on naturally to the substitution of writing for lecturing, which was daily proving more necessary, both for his own sake and for the world's, if the ideas which underlay his efforts to revive and popularise the English traditional dances were to receive permanent and authoritative expression.

After some preliminary compunction that he had undertaken a task which had to be completed within a given time, he entered into the work with zest. Long before I expected it, he sent me a draft of the whole book. I did not find, as had happened once before, that my whole service as collaborator would consist in overcoming his own diffidence about his writing and in urging him to leave well alone ; nor did he send me, as I had invited, mere disconnected notes to be converted into literary form. Substantially the draft stood as it is now. I returned it with my first crop of criticisms which, though some of them were very fundamental, he discussed with his invariable courtesy towards other points of view and his always astonishing patience in expounding his own. Quite soon he rewrote entirely the portion on the Spectacular Dance and sent it to me. He continued to work upon the earlier parts of the book with the idea of finishing it before the summer allowed him to resume his campaign of lecturing and judging competitions in the provinces. Then came his short and final illness. Until the very end he retained his interest in the book and the studies connected with it, hoping, even when other interests seemed to be passing from him, to be spared for more quiet research and exposition of the same kind in the future, but anxious about certain features in the book itself which, in my natural wish to make things easier for him, I did not ask him to specify.

When the remainder of the manuscript was returned to me after his death I found that he had revised it very carefully, rewriting certain passages and inserting fresh material. He had modified it to meet certain of my observations, strengthened it in places against others. Clearly he had no intention of rewriting it as he had the second portion, and if he contemplated making clear by means of a final summing up all that was not fully expressed in the book itself, and at the same time elaborating ideas which were scarcely even implicit in it, I am convinced from reading the drafts of it, all pathetically coming to an end at the same point, that it would never have been written, at any rate as a part of this book. Nor was it really needed. The manuscript was continuous with carefully prepared beginnings and endings and without a single gap. It could therefore fairly be regarded as complete—far more so than many books when they are first sent forward to be set up in type.

Yet no book can be said to be finished until the last proofs, with all their imperfections accepted as inevitable, have reluctantly been passed for press. Least of all could this be so with Cecil Sharp, who had a passion for scrupulous accuracy in detail and austere economy of diction, and yet had always to combat the lecturer's proneness to initial over-statement. When writing this book, too, he was seriously ill, and he relied on me for a close scrutiny from a friendly but totally different point of view. Sometimes, indeed, I seem to feel a direct personal challenge to an argument which, alas, can now never take place. I have therefore had no hesitation in altering the manuscript in places where for one concrete reason or another I feel satisfied that he would have accepted my criticism. As a rule, changing a word or the turn of a sentence has sufficed; only once has the correction of a mistranslation entailed considerable consequential modifications. Where, however, I know that he felt strongly I have changed or omitted nothing, even though I am unable to agree or fail to understand. Nor have I attempted, as we should certainly have done together, to secure, by additions here, excisions elsewhere, and by a general overhaul of parts a fuller emphasis to the principal points of the essay. In the Social Dance these are, as I take it, the origin in the peasantry—or, in his sense of the word, the folk—of every dance and its eventual decline and discontinuance when it had undergone for some time the processes of a conscious art; and, underlying these, a contrast and a comparison with the history of music for which, unlike the dance, a satisfactory system of notation insured continuity and permanence. In the account of the Spectacular Dance the main points seem to be its close association in the early days with social dances, its too complete absorption by virtuosity and the comparatively recent origin of the type of Ballet which is now regarded as the legitimate and traditional. To have re-fashioned the survey in order to bring out these points would

xii.

inevitably have demanded the curtailment in detail of the other feature which has in fact become predominant. I mean, of course, the importance to history of the English Country Dance. In other circumstances this would have been a mere postponement. Cecil Sharp would have returned to this theme more freely and amply in a separate book. But with no hope now of postponement, everyone will be glad that, even at the expense of balance in the book itself, he devoted so much space to the subject which was nearest to his heart and lay at the moment readiest to his hand.

In other ways too an unfinished sketch, or even rough, unshaped notes, may prove more stimulating than an elaborated work with all the reservations fully expressed and its proportions refined into perfect balance. This may well prove to be the case with this essay. The theme is anyhow so gigantic that no one could have attempted to exhaust it within the limits imposed. Nor can Cecil Sharp's point of view ever be ignored in any serious history of the dance unless, indeed, it be confined to the mimetic or "æsthetic" forms which, rightly or wrongly, he regarded as lying entirely outside his scope.

Many, perhaps most, of the illustrations had been provisionally chosen by us in consultation before Cecil Sharp fell ill. A few, such as the frontispiece to the *Ballet Comique de la Reine* (Plate 25), were entirely his choice. In most cases where I found specific reference to an illustration in his text it has proved possible, and indeed more convenient, to place it as a line-block on the page itself. As a rule, however, his interest in the picture or print was entirely free from pre-possessions in favour of any particular type of dance or even antiquarian considerations. He often lamented his want of trained appreciation of the arts of design, but he extended to them the discriminating delight in the simple, the direct and the beautiful which he showed for literature and music in all their forms and, indeed, despite his enforced asceticism for all the good things of life. Except that he could not reconcile himself to the representations of grotesque peasant dances by Dürer and his followers, although he recognised their monumental draughtsmanship and design, he seemed to care little what type of dance was represented, provided that the poise of the dancers was living and lightly portrayed or the balance and pattern of the design skilful. So catholic and unsectarian indeed was his taste that had he been given ten years more of life, this book might well have proved not, as it was intended, the prelude to his exposition of English traditional dance, but, rather, a second step, the first being his study of Thoinot-Arbeau, in the extension of his interests to other developments of the folk dance besides the English Country Dances.

However that might have been, Cecil Sharp did not reach the stage of close study and assimilation of the illustrations which would have accompanied their actual selection for the book. I have therefore been very sparing in inserting fresh references to plates in the text. Even a slight difference between the date of the picture and the period mentioned in the text might make the reference misleading. Dances undergo such rapid transformation that even though the name and the tune may remain the same, it would be dangerous to argue full identity even over a comparatively short term of years. Possibly the process was slower in old days than at present but, even so, the Saraband in the *Ballet des Ridicules* of 1628 (Plate 32) has no apparent connection with the dances of that name mentioned in the text, and the relation between Playford's Country Dances and Hogarth's (Plate 47) or Rowlandson's (Plate 2) must have been comparatively remote. It is not, however, as representations of the actual postures or movements of the dances that the illustrations are primarily valuable. From the nature of the case they can only be approximate, and even the best of them are open to such criticisms from the technical point of view as were made on the appearance of Lancret's Mademoiselle Camargo (Plate 43), though it is apparently intended, and certainly is generally accepted, as a careful representation. It is much less for this that they should be studied than for the light that they throw upon the spirit of the dance, the bearing and character of the performers, the background and the concomitants of costume, furniture and scenery and, sometimes, for their own intrinsic merits as works of art. For this their arrangement in chronological order and the strict exclusion of all reconstructions or imaginary dances, ancient or modern, should suffice, without elaborate references from text to illustration.

I regret that I am unable to record the names of all the friends and authorities to whom Cecil Sharp would have wished to proclaim his indebtedness. I know that he owed much to his constant associate and fellow-worker, Miss Maud Karpeles, who helped him in this book, as always, in every conceivable way in which an author can be assisted; and to Mrs. Shuldham Shaw, who had furnished him with material of a historical character for years before this book was undertaken. I know, too, that he had fruitful conversations about it with Mr. Kennedy North and Mr. C. W. Beaumont. To all these I also acknowledge my indebtedness. I have consulted Miss Karpeles about all, or nearly all, my modifications in the manuscript and she has concurred in them. She has also verified from Cecil Sharp's note-books many points of which I was doubtful. Mrs. Shaw's accurate and full notes of drawings and prints in Paris were of the greatest assistance to me. Besides these, I owe a debt of gratitude for constant help and courtesy to Messrs. Hake, Eric Millar, Walters, Martin Hardie and Craster and their assistants in the departments of Prints and Drawings, Manuscripts and Classical Antiquities of

PREFACE

the British Museum, Engraving Illustration and Design of the Victoria and Albert Museum and the Bodleian Library. Mr. Edward Clayton, of Messrs. Agnews, has helped me very greatly with his knowledge of French prints and drawings; and for information and assistance generally or with regard to particular plates, I am also indebted to Mrs. Arthur Strong and Mademoiselle Edith Silz, Sir Robert Witt, Dr. Lionel Cust, Professor Borenius and Dr. K. T. Parker. Gratitude is also due to the many owners of prints, pictures and drawings who have been so good as to give us permission to reproduce them. Their names are in each case recorded under the plate itself.

A. P. OPPÉ.

INTRODUCTION—THE FOLK DANCE.

INTRODUCTION—THE FOLK DANCE.

IN the course of its evolution the dance, like music and certain other forms of human expression, has passed through two more or less clearly defined phases. Originally, it was an instinctive, spontaneous, communal utterance due to the desire on the part of a tribe or community to give concrete expression to spiritual conceptions, aspirations and ideals, felt and held in common. Later on, as the corporate bond weakened, the community broke up into its elements and became less homogeneous. The development of the dance, hitherto the unconscious concern of the community, gradually fell into the hands of individuals who consciously modified existing communal forms. The basis of the dance, therefore, is unconscious and racial; its super-structure conscious and individual.

We shall find, however, that in the dance the transference of the creative impulse from the community to the individual has been less complete or, at any rate, less evident, than in other arts—music, for instance. It will, however, be possible, I think, to show that this transference did take place, even though the individuals into whose hands the development of the dance ultimately fell cannot always be identified, and their names, when recorded, belong very often to comparatively humble and undistinguished persons—dancing-masters, Court Chamberlains, and the like.

Approaching the history of the dance in this way, we stand at the outset of our enquiry upon solid ground; for the racial or folk-dance still survives in various forms in the several nations of Europe, and its peculiarities and characteristics can be observed and noted. Equipped with this knowledge as a preliminary the task of the historian is greatly simplified. He has but to examine critically, and review the value and significance of, the attempts that from time to time have been made to develop the dance beyond the point to which the folk had carried it. This would not have been a task of insuperable difficulty if the results of these successive efforts had been accurately recorded. But, unhappily, this is not so. Except for a very complex stenographic system used in the choreography of the ballet, and that by experts only, there is, even now, no universal nor moderately satisfactory system of dance notation; each composer has very largely to construct his own, which is inevitably cumbrous and very rarely intelligible to anyone but himself and his immediate coadjutors. Consequently, while the music and songs of a popular work can be printed and made known to thousands who are unable to hear them at the theatre, there is no way by which a similar knowledge of the dances can be disseminated.

On this account, the task of the historian of the dance is one of especial and peculiar difficulty; his researches will be hampered at every turn by the almost complete absence of any trustworthy record of past achievements of composers of the dance. That the historian should be embarrassed by this defect is, however, a matter of comparative unimportance: infinitely more serious is the obstruction from this cause to the normal development of the art itself, even though we allow some compensating advantage to the absence of the " dead hand." For composers have not only been unable to record their own compositions for the benefit of posterity, but have been debarred from studying the experiments of their predecessors. The compositions of individual composers have been isolated and unrelated to anything but the work of their contemporaries; there has been no cumulative progress. The effect of this may be seen in the fact—not usually realised—that the past history of the dance contains the name of scarcely a single composer of acknowledged repute. To recite the names of the great musicians from John of Dunstable to Richard Wagner is to pass mentally in review the history and progress of music. But in the whole history of the dance there are no more than two or three composers whose names have come down to us, and even these we know by contemporary report, not—except in a very few cases—by their actual achievements.

The dance, consequently, has never come into its full estate, but has remained throughout its history in the fluid, indeterminate state of the folk-dance, always approaching finality by means of continuous, imperceptible changes, but never reaching it in the form of a defined, unalterable composition. In other respects the dance has long since entered upon the second, non-folk, stage of its evolution, and fallen under the influence of cultivated people. These two aspects in its development—the maintenance of a fluid, indeterminate state, while subject to sophisticated influence—are clearly to be seen in the evolution of the jazz during the last few years.

The reader, therefore, must not expect a continuous narrative, an orderly series of documents. All that can be put before him are the larger facts and the broader tendencies which have shaped the course of the dance. With our first step, however—the examination of folk-dance—we stand on comparatively firm ground.

A detailed, technical, description of the European folk-dance would take up more space than can be spared in this short sketch; a short, general account will, however, suffice for our purpose.

All the nations of Europe have their own distinctive forms of folk-dance, some in a purer form than others. Many of these have not been collected, and are not therefore as yet available to the student. The folk-dances of England and of a few other nations have, however, been noted and published, and from them it is possible to discern the general character and the lines along which all have developed. The earliest forms of folk-dance bear upon them unmistakable signs of a religious origin; indeed, some of them are still performed ritually, as pagan ceremonies of a quasi-religious or magic character, usually

4

associated with the cultivation and fertility of the soil, and performed at particular seasons of the year. English folk-dances may be placed in three categories—the Sword Dance, Morris Dance, and Country Dance. Of these the first two are the more important, in that they exhibit comparatively few signs of sophistication, for although the Morris, and to a lesser degree the Sword Dance, have from time to time been danced and exploited by the middle and upper classes, the peasantry in some part or other of the country have never, until quite recently, given up the traditional habit of performing them ritually and ceremonially, each at its own proper season of the year.

The Sword Dance is a highly elaborate, complex figure-dance, executed with very simple steps in ring-formation, by five, six or more men, each holding a sword in his right hand and clasping the tip of the sword of his left neighbour. In this restricted formation a large number of intricate figures are performed, the dancers leaping, or turning back-somersaults, over their swords, passing under them, twisting and turning in every imaginable way without breaking the essential ring-formation. The dance culminates with the weaving of the swords into a tight knot, in shape a polygonal figure, known as the Glass, Knot, or Lock, which is placed round the neck of one of the performers or, more often, one of the bystanders, who suffers a mimic decapitation by the drawing of the swords. Sometimes, each of the dancers, in turn, is crowned with the lock; in other variants two dancers are raised upon separate Locks and engage in mimic warfare (Plate 18); but more usually the Lock is used as an instrument of death. In England the dance is performed annually between Christmas and the New Year and symbolizes the death of the Old Year and, when the victim, as occasionally happens, is brought to life again, the birth of the New Year.

In the Morris Dance, which appears to have been evolved from the Sword Dance, the dancers have discarded the sword and carry sticks or handkerchiefs. Like the Sword Dancers, the Morris men, six in number, are dressed in ritual costume, gay with bright coloured ribbons, rosettes, flowers and greenery. They wear a pad of bells on each leg. The Morris, unlike the Sword Dance, is essentially a step dance with highly developed foot, hand, and body movements, its figures being few in number and comparatively simple in character. It is danced at the Spring time of the year, usually during Whitsun week, to the accompaniment—till a few years ago—of the pipe-and-tabor. It used to be the custom—and still is in some parts of England—for the Morris Dancers to blacken their faces. This to our fifteenth-century ancestors made them look like Moors, and it has been suggested that this led to the dance being called the Morisco—hence Morris.

The Morris and Sword Dances are, or were, to be found in most of the countries of Europe, though they appear to have survived more perfectly and more generally in England, where more than a hundred

5

different varieties of the former and twenty of the latter have been collected and published.

The third type, the Country Dance, differs from the other two in that it is danced by men and women in couples, instead of by men only, and perhaps for this reason has developed into a social dance. It was derived from the Mayday dance, which is still to be seen in England and in many parts of Europe, in both its forms, the Processional dances and the rounds, of which that around the May-tree or pole is, perhaps, the better known.

It is commonly assumed that the folk-dance, being the invention of primitive, unlettered, country people, is necessarily of a very simple, embryonic type, and that peasant dancers are crude, uncouth, heavy-footed performers, making up for their lack of technique by an unrestrained exuberance; in this way, indeed, they have always been represented in pictures. But this is by no means in accordance with fact, as those who, like the writer, have been in close touch with genuine traditional dancers, are in a position to testify. Some folk-dances are no doubt simple enough; and these perhaps are the most valuable, for they are the basic elemental types from which the more complex have been derived. On the other hand, many folk-dances are extremely complex, highly developed in structure as well as in their steps, movements and figures. The expert drawing-room dancer would be hard put to it to memorise a Morris or Sword Dance, or to execute either with the dexterity, the force, and at the same time, with the restraint of the best folk-dancers; or, again, to acquire the technique of that easy swaying movement of the body, akin to that of the skater, which is the peculiar accomplishment of all folk-dancers. It would probably be

Fig. (a) *Dancers from the manuscript of the Alexander Romance (14th cent.)*
in the Bodleian Library.

6

nearer the truth to assert that no form of art has been carried so far along the road of development by the unaided efforts of the folk as that of the dance.

This, very shortly, is the nature of the racial dance, strictly conditioned in its range but neither embryonic nor imperfectly developed, upon which, as a foundation, the cultivated art has been built.

SOCIAL DANCE.

SOCIAL DANCE.

There is no ancient civilisation of which we have any record that did not know dancing; the Egyptians, Assyrians, Hebrews, Hindus, Greeks, Romans, all practised it. No nation, indeed, held dancing in higher esteem, or cultivated it for its ethical and æsthetic values more generally and more seriously than the ancient Greeks; and did we possess any accurate information concerning their dances, were we able to reproduce but a single one of them, the addition to our knowledge and understanding of the early history of the art would be immeasurable. But unhappily this knowledge is not, and never can be, ours, for the Greeks had no method of notation by which they could transmit their dances to posterity, and consequently we are unable to reconstruct so much as one isolated phrase. M. Maurice Emmanuel, by a patient and exhaustive examination of the dance-figures depicted on Greek vases, claims to have identified many of the steps and gestures used by Greek dancers with those in use in the modern ballet. But even though his conclusions were unassailable, as of course in the nature of things they cannot be, this would not carry us very far. For isolated steps and postures are merely the raw material, the vocabulary of the dance, and have no significance unless, and until, they are combined into rhythmical phrases or sentences and associated with their musical accompaniment. The so-called Classical Dancing of the present day is the veriest guess-work, apart from some of the individual static gestures and attitudes, and the flowing robes, sandalled feet and filletted heads of the executants.

That the Greek dances were based upon the indigenous dances of the common people who lived around them there can be little doubt; indeed, this may be inferred from the likeness which some of the drawings on the vases bear to folk-dances still in use in modern Greece and other European countries. The Farandole repeatedly occurs through its suitability for decoration, and the step depicted in figure c is that of a well-known folk-dance used by the peasants of several countries including our own.

Fig. (b) Salome Dancing. From a manuscript (12th cent.) in the Bodleian Library.

At its best, Roman dancing probably approximated to that of Greece, partly through being derived from it and probably through being based on analogous indigenous traditions; at its worst we know that it fell far below and, in the latter days of the Empire, became incredibly coarse, licentious and degenerate. The Romans, however, instituted and developed dancing in the theatre, and

11

the invention of Pantomime must be credited to ancient Italy.

Very little is known about European dancing during the dark centuries that followed the fall of the Roman Empire. Dancing in Saxon England as practised by the gleemen and minstrels, that is, professional as distinct from social or folk-dancing, consisted, judging by contemporary drawings, mainly of acrobatic feats, tumbling, balancing and other gymnastic tricks. These were performed very largely by women, the *tomblesteres* and *tombesteres* of Chaucer, also called *saylours* (from *salio*) and *sauters*, *i.e.*, leapers and jumpers. In Saxon

Fig. (c) *Satyrs Dancing. From a Pompeian Wall Painting, 1st Century A.D.*
(Museo Borbonico, vii. 50).

versions of St. Mark's Gospel it is said of the daughter of Herodias that " she vaulted or tumbled " before King Herod, or she " tomblyde and pleside Harrowde." In this way she is depicted in many illuminations of early manuscripts. The most curious of these is, perhaps, the miniature from a manuscript of the 12th century in the Bodleian Library (figure *b*), in which Salome combines her normal " tumbling " attitude with extraordinary feats of juggling with swords. In an earlier representation, reproduced by Strutt as from an Anglo-Saxon manuscript (figure *d*), the step is identical with one found on Greek vases, etc. (figure *c*), to which reference has already been made. I have often

12

seen it danced in Somerset and Devon, where it is called the Kibby or Monkey dance. It is an acrobatic feat calling for great agility, the performer crouching on his haunches and alternately throwing forward his legs. Thus this very characteristic step was danced in Greece five centuries before our era, in Saxon England of the tenth century, and still survives in the twentieth century—a remarkable instance of the persistence of tradition.

Fig. (d)   The Kibby-Dance
(from Strutt).

XVI. CENTURY.

Several centuries must be crossed before we reach the firm ground of documentary evidence. The first dances of which we possess technical information, at once intelligible, detailed and trustworthy, are the Basse dances and the Pavanes. The former flourished from about 1350 to 1550, and the latter from 1450 to the middle of the seventeenth century. The earliest written description of the Basse dance is in a Burgundian MS. of the 14th century, *Le livre des basse-danses;* then come an Italian MS. by Gulielmus Hebraeus of Pesaro (1416); an English description translated from the French and appended to a treatise on the French language by Robert Coplande (1521); an Italian treatise, *Il Ballarino,* by Fabritio Caroso (1581); and finally, the account in Thoinot Arbeau's *Orchésographie* (1588).

The description given by Arbeau, or to give him his real name and title, Jehan Tabourot, Abbé of Lengres, is, though the fullest, the latest in date, but he was 69 years of age when he wrote his book, and was old enough, therefore, to have danced both the Basse dances and the Pavanes in his youth, and actually did so. Moreover, though Caroso's account is extremely interesting and in some respects more detailed, he did not possess the gift of exposition to the same degree as Arbeau, whose account must accordingly be followed as the clearest. The Basse dance, according to Arbeau, was danced *par terre,* that is, without springing off the floor, a walking not a running movement. It was a very slow, dignified dance, one step to each measure of three minims. The movements, each of which took four measures to perform, were five in number: the double (three steps and feet-together); two simples (a step and feet-together, repeated); the branle (an elaborate four-fold honour); the reprise (a curious shaking step on alternate feet, executed four times); and the révérence (a single, impressive bow or courtesy). The dance consisted of three separate and distinct parts—the Basse

13

dance proper, the Retour of the Basse dance, and the Tordion. This is the formula of the first part, as given by Arbeau, the movements being indicated by their initial letters, a capital R distinguishing the révérence from the reprise—R b ss d r d r b ss ddd r d r b ss d r b c (congé).

The Retour was a shortened form of the Basse dance proper performed with the same steps and movements but arranged in a different order.

The third part, the Tordion, was quite different in character as well as in steps and movements, and was in reality a modified form of the Galliard, with which it will presently be described.

The Pavane, like the Basse dance, was a formal, stately dance with gliding steps, *par terre*, but performed to rather a faster tempo and without the elaborate honours of the Basse dance. It consisted of two simples followed by a double, executed four times in the 32 bars of the tune, one step to each measure of two minims. The dance is said to have come from Padua, and it is often called Paduane, Paduana, or Pavana. Some, however, derive it from *pavo*, a peacock, from the way in which the ladies preened the trains of their dresses and the cavaliers strutted by their sides, thrusting back their cloaks with their swords. Both Pavane and Basse dance were danced in couples, very often, but not necessarily, in procession. The dance depicted in Plate 19 is almost certainly one or other of these two dances.

Those who are acquainted with the Helston Furry and the Tideswell dances of England or the Polonaise of Poland will not hesitate to relate both Basse dance and Pavane to the May dance in its processional form, though in the passage from country-side to Court they shed many of their most characteristic qualities. Indeed, their portentous solemnity, their formal, spiritless movements, above all the self-conscious air with which they were performed, provide the very antithesis to the folk-dance. An interesting parallel might be drawn between these two dances and the early composed music known as the *organum*, which is equally far removed from folk-music. Sir John Davies in a couplet in his *Orchestra* (1596), the earliest dance-poem in our language, gives, perhaps, the reason :—

> But after these, as men more civill grew
> He did more grave and solemn measures frame,

and he seems to refer to the Pavane in the lines :—

> Yet all the feete whereon these measures goe,
> Are only Spondeis, solemn, grave and sloe.

The Galliard, another dance described by Arbeau, is very ancient, dating certainly from the fifteenth century, and even from the fourteenth, if the Tordion formed part of the Basse dance at that time. It is said to have originated in Rome—hence the name *Romanesca* by which it was known in Italy. Unlike the two dances just described, the

14

FLANDERS. XVI. CENTURY.

PLATE 1.

THE TORCH DANCE FROM A BOOK OF HOURS (THE " GOLF BOOK ").
PROBABLY BY SIMON BENING. SCHOOL OF BRUGES.

(British Museum).

Galliard was a Haute Danse, or Danse Balladine, that is, it was danced with springing not gliding steps. As its name implies it was a lively, spirited dance and, it may be added, very complex, with steps far more varied and difficult than those of the Basse dance or Pavane. In its simplest and most elemental form it consisted of a short phrase of two bars of music in 3/2 time, that is, six minims, to which five steps were performed, the dancer springing into the air off his fourth step, missing the fifth minim, and alighting on the sixth and last note. On this account the dance was often known as the cinq-pas—the cinque-pace or sinkapace of Shakespeare. Arbeau describes in great detail a dozen or more steps that were used in the dance and several ways in which these might be combined in passages of varying lengths, or *enchaînements*, as they would be called now. The Grand Saut—sometimes a Capriol—followed by the " posture " on the sixth minim, was the outstanding feature of the dance; but this, Arbeau tells us, might, at the discretion of the dancer, be omitted and the cadence, which it formed, be postponed to the end of the 4th, 6th, 8th, 10th, or even later bar.

The tune of our National Anthem is in form a Galliard, in which the Grand Saut would be made off the dotted note at the beginning of the second and every alternate bar. The Sherborne Jig, well-known to Morris dancers, is also a true Galliard; indeed, nearly all of the steps which Arbeau tells us were used in this dance are steps that are still danced by English Morris men. Here, therefore, we have a definite and, we may add, a very beautiful derivate of the traditional Morris. The dancers of those days must have been very skilful executants, for many of the passages which Arbeau notes, still more those which he tells us the dancers improvised, present considerable technical difficulty.

Galliards were danced in couples holding inside hands. The dance would begin quietly, with simple steps, once or twice round the room, after which the man would take his partner to one end of the hall and dance before her, exhibiting his best steps and passages; then, taking her by the hand, he would dance down to the other end of the room and repeat the process, and so on. The Galliard was therefore of the nature of a solo dance though nominally a double one.

The Tordion was danced with the same steps as the Galliard but more quietly, without spring, and omitting the more elaborate passages and steps, each couple holding hands throughout and dancing round, or up and down, the room.

The Galliard was usually danced directly after the Pavane, and musicians often coupled the two dances together, as, for instance, Bull (1562-1628) in his " Pavane and Galliard." There are 26 Pavanes and Galliards *en suite* in the Fitzwilliam virginal book. Morley, too, describes the Galliard as " a kind of music made out of the other (*i.e.*, the Pavane), a lighter and more stirring dance than the Pavane, and consisting of the same number of straines."

15

It was, we may assume, the slow, formal, solemn character of the Basse dances that led to their discontinuance in the middle of the 16th century. At any rate, the dances that came into fashion in their place —Arbeau calls them "new dances"—were altogether more varied, brighter, livelier and more closely related to the country-dances from which they were evidently derived. No less than twenty-nine of these dances are described by Arbeau, the Branle in twenty-three varieties, the Volta, Courante, Allemande, Gavotte, Canaries, and the Pavane d'Espagne. The first four Branles, the Double, Single, Gay and Bourgogne Branles, are obviously derivates of the May processional dance, and bear some relation to the Basse dance, though less formal, being without pauses for honours and reverences, and consequently more sociable. Arbeau says that all the balls of his day began with these; staid, middle-aged dancers tread with dignified mien the Double and Single Branles; young married couples the Gay Branle; and the demoiselles and young bachelors the Branles of Bourgogne. After this formal beginning the new dances, including the other Branles, were performed. Many of the latter are "miming" Branles, that is, action-dances, mildly dramatic, very similar to our singing-games (although, apparently, the dancers did not sing the tunes), e.g., the Branles des Hermites, de Malte, des Lavandières (cf. The Mulberry Bush), des Pois, du Chandelier (or de la Torche), des Sabots, des Chevaux, etc. Other Branles described by Arbeau are called by the name of the town or province from which they were derived, such as the Branles de Bourgogne, du Hault Barrois, de Poictou, d'Ecosse, de Bretagne. Finally, there are the Branles Couppées, in suites of ten or more numbers, in which half-steps, fleurets, and other decorative steps, borrowed from the Galliard, were introduced according to the fancy of the dancer. The Branles, with the exception of the Branles Couppées, are closely related to the folk-dance; some of them—the games, for instance—are almost pure folk-dances; the term Branle, in English Brawl, seems to have been a generic term applied to all dances which were quasi-folk in character.

The Volta (also written volte, lavolta) came from Provence, and was a species of Galliard in that it was danced in two bars of triple time and culminated with a leap. It was danced by a man and his partner revolving in a small circle. It begins with two preliminary steps, a short and a long, on the first two beats of the first bar, the man holding his partner's hand; on the third beat the man seizes his partner and lifts her into the air the dancer alighting on the first beat of the second bar and resting for the two following beats. Arbeau gives minute directions for the way in which the man must handle his partner to lift her, and the way in which she must support herself upon him and incidentally keep her skirts in place. It was a most exhausting dance and, in Arbeau's opinion, indelicate and unseemly. Apparently, the turning

16

was executed on the spot without moving round the room as in the waltz, for Arbeau says that at the end of four turns (each three-quarter way round) the dancers should be in the place from which they started and facing in the same direction. Sir John Davies describes this dance in the words :—

> Yet is there one the most delightfull kind,
> A loftie jumping, or a leaping round,
> Where arme in arme, two Dauncers are entwind,
> And whirle themselves with strickt embracements bound
> And still their feet an Anapest doe sound.

By "Anapest" he means the two short preliminary steps and the following leap and pause. The Volta was popular in England, but, apparently, not for long, since it is rarely mentioned after the early years of the seventeenth century.

The Courante as described by Arbeau was a quick dance in 2-time, consisting of two Simples and a Double to the left and then to the right, the dancers in couples going forward, backward, or to the side, as they pleased. The steps were quick and light with springs from foot to foot. Ordinarily the man held the left hand of his partner in his right throughout the dance, but he would sometimes leave hold of her, execute a short *pas seul* with a "turn single," and then return to her again. Sir John Davies probably referred to the Courante when he talked of those "currant travases," and Shakespeare hits off the character of this and the dance which has just been described when he makes Bourbon in Henry V. say :—

> They bid us to the English dancing schools
> And teach lavoltas high and swift corantos.

The Courante, as well as the Gavotte and other double dances, was often performed in processional formation.

The Allemande, according to Arbeau, came from Germany, and was therefore, he said, to be accounted of ancient origin, for "we are descended from the Germans." It was danced to the Morris step, both 4/3 and 4/2, in couples ranged one behind the other, and was divided into three parts by short intervals, during which the dancers engaged in conversation. In the third part the duration of each step was doubled in length as in the Capers of the Morris. The characteristic arm-positions of the Allemandes of the 17th and 18th centuries (see Plates 52 & 54) were, apparently, a later development.

Arbeau derives the Gavotte from the Double Branle, and says that it was danced in 2-time, in springing steps, with Doubles to the right and left alternately. The dancers, however, were in the habit of "dividing" their steps, substituting faster and more decorative footing for the straightforward normal steps of the double. After the dancers had danced for some little while the leading couple would separate from the rest, and dance several passages in the middle of the room in full view

17

of the other dancers. Having finished these passages the man kissed his partner, and then proceeded to kiss all the other ladies in turn, while his partner treated the men in like manner. This procedure was repeated until each couple, in turn, had led the dance.

The Passa-mezzo is by some believed to have been so named because it was danced down the middle of the room, but Arbeau says that when a Pavane was danced less deliberately and to a faster tempo, it became very much like a Basse dance and was then called a Passa-mezzo (*i.e.*, in half-steps).

The "Canaries" Dance is derived by Arbeau from a ballet-masquerade, in which the dancers were dressed as kings and queens of Mauretania, or as savages with plumes of many colours. In dancing, partners stood *vis-à-vis* at opposite ends of the room and each, alternately, danced toward the other and then back to his place. In the execution of these passages the dancers were expected to introduce strange and bizarre steps "such as savages would use," and to do this had to draw upon their powers of improvisation. Arbeau describes one of these characteristic passages, and suggests ways in which others could be devised. The Pavane d'Espagne was, he says, similar.

Arbeau also describes two dances, the Morisque and Les Bouffons, which were for men only and therefore not social dances. We know them to be folk-dances; the former a Morris Jig, the latter a form of Sword Dance. The Morisque, he says, was often danced at good houses after supper by a single performer with blackened face, a band of white or yellow taffeta round his forehead, and bells on his legs. Thus equipped, he dances up and down the hall using various steps, one of which Arbeau notes. This step is not the normal Morris step, similar to that danced in the Allemande, but a curious, heel-and-toe movement which, strange to relate, I once noted from a Morris dancer in a Northamptonshire village. I have never seen anyone else dance this step, but the fact that Arbeau saw it danced in France nearly 300 years ago proves, I think, that it is a genuine tradition.

Les Bouffons differs in many respects from the English Sword Dance, though here, again, are some startling similarities, such as the mode of calling upon a dancer to take his place in the dance by scraping the sword on the ground at his feet.

There were other dances in France and elsewhere in the sixteenth century which are not mentioned by Arbeau, such as the Bourrée, a peasant dance of the Auvergne, which was not fully accepted at Court, probably because of its characteristic stamping of feet, though it is said to have been introduced there by Marguerite of Valois; the Passepied, which was a sailor's dance from Basse Bretagne; the Rigaudon, a lively little dance from Provence or Languedoc, which became very popular in England towards the end of the 17th century, and is included in Feuillet's *Chorégraphie*; the Chaconne, which came from Spain, and

18

the Passecaille, from the same country or from Italy. Perhaps the best known of these is the Saraband, which is also said by some to have originated in Spain in the 16th century, though others give it an Eastern origin. The ugly, coarse movements and the lascivious words of the song to which it was danced give weight to this ascription. The dance in its original form was so objectionable that it was for a time suppressed by Philip II. It found its way, greatly purified, into the French Court at the latter end of the 16th century. Originally it is said to have been a solo dance, performed by a woman while singing and accompanying herself on the guitar. It was a favourite dance of Charles II., and Grammont ridicules the popularity of a Saraband air with his fellow-courtiers. The dance disappeared in the early years of the 18th century. J. J. Rousseau (*Les Pensées*, 1772) says that it was not danced in his day except occasionally in opera.

But of none of these dances have we so clear an idea as of those described by Arbeau. For he had not only an intimate knowledge of the social dances of his day, having danced them himself, but an acute, technical mind and the rare gift of lucid exposition. It would be difficult to exaggerate the historical importance of his treatise, for it contains all the exact knowledge that we have of the dances of the 15th and 16th centuries.

Many of these dances were danced at the Court of Elizabeth. In addition to them, English people were dancing at this period their own Country Dances. Although we have to wait for technical information concerning these until the publication of Playford's *English Dancing Master* (1650), there is no doubt but that they were danced in 16th century England, and probably earlier. Dances of the advanced character that many of the Playford dances display were not the growth of a day but the fruit of a development extending over many generations. Moreover, three of the dances, The Vicar of St. Fools, Putney Ferry and The Shaking of the Sheets (also known as The Dede Dance) are mentioned in *Misogonus* a comedy dating from about 1560; and mentioned, too, quite casually as ordinary and popular dances of the day. The Dede Dance and Putney Ferry are both described in *The Dancing-Master*, while the former is included in the list of dances given in the *Complaynt of Scotland* (1548), and is mentioned in Gosson's *Schoole of Abuse* (1579). In the form given by Playford, it is one of the more advanced Country Dances.

By the end of the century the Country Dance had penetrated into the Court, for the Earl of Worcester writes to the Earl of Salisbury in 1602: "We all frolic here at Court; much dancing in the Privy Chamber of country dances before the Queen's Majesty, who is exceedingly pleased therewith." The country dances, however, did not compete with the Brawles, Courantes and other French dances at any rate at Court, nor probably in polite society, but appear to have been danced

19

at the end of the evening after the first formalities had worn off and the need was felt of some lighter form of enjoyment. Where, however, they flourished most was amongst the middle classes of the kingdom, and of course in the social life of the villages, at fairs, merry-makings, Bride-ales and similar functions (Plate 24).

The English Dancing-Master, from which all our technical knowledge of these dances is derived, was published by John Playford in 1650, and, under the title of *The Dancing-Master*, subsequently went through eighteen editions, covering a period of nearly eighty years, *i.e.*, down to 1728. The original book contained 104 dances; the last edition, in three volumes, nearly 900. The dances described are of several kinds; Ring-dances or Rounds, Square-eights, dances for two couples *vis-à-vis*, and Longways dances (partners facing one another in two files) for three or four couples, or "for as many as will." The steps of the Country Dance are quite simple, merely running, slipping or skipping movements, the dance depending for its expressiveness upon elaborate figure evolutions. Of the dances in the first edition some are folk-dances, pure and simple; the rest represent various degrees of development, and include several which testify to the existence at that time of extremely skilful composers, and, for some of them are very difficult, of skilled executants also. Who these composers were we can only guess, for Playford does not record their names, but there were many skilled dance composers in England at that time some of whose names are known in connection with the Masque dance, *e.g.*, Frith, Giles, Confess, etc., and we may safely assume that they were responsible for some of the country dances.

The Country Dance, then, was essentially a figure-dance, and in this respect it is sharply to be distinguished from all the dances so far described. That other countries besides England had folk-dances of a similar type there can be little doubt, but in no other nation were they developed nor danced by all classes of the community as they undoubtedly were in this country.

If the dances of the 16th century are considered critically it will be seen that two of them, the Galliard and the English Country Dance, stand out pre-eminently. The Branles, Corantos, Gavottes, etc., delightful as many of them are, especially in their early forms, represent, nevertheless, but a small advance upon the folk-dance. On the other hand, the Galliard and Country Dance, while retaining the essential qualities of the folk-dance, display considerable development, the former in the elaboration of step, the latter in that of concerted figure-movements. Though nominally a double dance, the Galliard was virtually a solo, and its interest centred in the steps and leg-movements, which were unrelieved and unaided by any of the arm and body-movements which are so characteristic a feature of its progenitor, the Morris Dance.

20

The Country Dance, on the other hand, presented the dancer with no technical difficulties of any moment, though it demanded of him a delicate poise and balance of body and deft foot-work in order to control speed and direction of motion in the execution of the figures, which were very numerous, varied and often very intricate. It was essentially a concerted dance requiring at least four performers, varied in structure, in content, and in the character of its accompanying music. It was instinct with the joyous spirit of the dance and, at a time when Court-dancers in France and Italy were treading their measures to grave, serious music, hardly to be distinguished from that which accompanied the Services of the Church, Courtiers in England were dancing to bright, jolly, rhythmical tunes, almost infinite in number and variety. Hitherto, the Country Dance has received but scant recognition from historians, owing partly to the obscure language in which the directions in *The English Dancing-Master* are couched, and the consequent difficulty in deciphering them. Now that the dances have been interpreted and translated into ordinary language, the historical significance and the artistic value of the contribution made by the English people at this period will, it is hoped, receive more general recognition.

XVII. CENTURY.

The country dances and Playford have taken us, in England, well into the 17th century. On the Continent that century was singularly barren in the invention of fresh dances. With the exception of the Minuet, which did not come into general use until the following century, no dances of any note were added to the repertory of the ball-room. This is not to say that interest in the dance declined during this period; on the contrary, it increased very greatly, but it was concentrated on the improvement of technique, the perfecting of style and manner of execution, rather than upon the enlargement of the stock of existing material.

During the first half of the century the Pavane fell into disfavour, and a like fate overtook the Galliard, owing partly to its executive difficulties, but mainly to the lively, animated character of the dance, which was in sharp conflict with the prevailing taste of the European Courts. The Volta, judged indecorous by Louis XIII., was summarily banished from the French Court.

The centre of the dance in Europe was the French Court, especially in the latter half of the century. Louis XIV. was an enthusiastic patron of the dance and no mean performer himself; he not only played a leading part at the Court balls and ceremonies, but in his younger days acted and danced in the royal opera-ballets. His favourite dance was the Courante, in which, it is recorded, he had a lesson every week from Beauchamps or Pécour, the Court dancing-masters.

The double Branle still held pride of place as the opening dance at Court functions, a position which it retained down to the middle of the 18th century; followed, as in the previous century, by Corantos, Gavottes and other Court dances. These latter dances, originally introduced, it will be remembered, because of their brightness and freshness, grew more and more formal, ceremonious and affected as the century advanced, until ultimately they became little more than exercises in deportment.

In the 16th century, dancers, other than those who cultivated the Galliard, seem to have troubled themselves but little with technicalities, but at Louis XIV.'s Court more attention was paid to technique. Steps and movements were analysed and systematised, and the dancing-master became a very important personage. The first and chief dance-instructor of the day was Beauchamps, a man of great ability and of original mind, the director of the royal school of dancing established by the King in 1661. He was the first to teach the " Five Positions," which to this day are still accepted as the basis of dance-technique. He was also proclaimed by a Decree of Parliament to be the inventor of a very elaborate system of choreography, which was asserted to be based upon the method used by Thoinot Arbeau, although they do not seem to have had anything in common. Beauchamps himself published nothing, but his system was explained in a treatise by Feuillet (1701), which was translated into English by Weaver five years later. This highly ingenious system had a vogue for a while but, owing to its exceeding complexity its practical value was small, and it fell into disuse in the course of a few years.

Beauchamps, again, was responsible for the Minuet, which it is believed he evolved from a folk-dance hailing from Poitou, possibly the Branle de Poictou described by Arbeau. It derived its name from the small (menu) steps, the chief characteristic of the dance in its original form. Grammont in his memoirs (1662-4) mentions that the Minuet was introduced into the English Court by a visitor from France, the Marquis de Flamarens, but it was many years before it became a recognised Court dance.

In England throughout this century the popularity of the Country Dance amongst all classes of the kingdom continued unabated, and this despite Puritan abuse. *The English Dancing-Master* was published little more than three years before the Commonwealth, the very time when the Puritans were most fiercely denouncing not only dancing, but all forms of artistic enjoyment. That a second edition of this popular book was called for within two years is proof that the Puritan preachers had not succeeded in suppressing dancing as completely as is commonly supposed.

22

Fig. (e)   Costume of Dancer, temp. Louis XIV., from a print.

In an interesting passage of his Diary, Pepys describes the procedure at a Court ball which he witnessed at Whitehall in 1662. As in
France it began with the Branle. "After that," he writes, "the King
led a lady a single Coranto ; and then the rest of the lords, one after
another, other ladies ; very noble it was, and a great pleasure to see.
Then to country dances ; the King leading the first, which he called for ;
which was, says he, 'Cuckolds all awry,' the old dance of England."
This dance, which was in all the earlier editions of *The Dancing-Master*,
is a dance "for foure," one of the older forms of the Country Dance.
   It is clear that although the French dances were performed at the
English Court, and, no doubt, in the stilted way in which they were now
being danced in France, they were followed, as in the days of Elizabeth,
by Country Dances. An examination of the successive editions of *The
Dancing-Master* between 1650 and 1698, however, shows that the more
formal Longways Country Dance was steadily displacing the earlier and
less conventional Rounds, Square-eights, etc. This decline from
popular favour of the older forms of the dance was possibly due in some

23

degree to French influence, but more probably to the increasing popularity of the Country Dance in more fashionable assemblies. Hitherto, the Country Dance had been regarded less as a rival than as an agreeable alternative, a refreshing contrast, to the more formal Court dances of polite society. But it is evident that during the latter years of this century it was beginning to challenge on its own merits the supremacy of its rivals, and it could do this more successfully by means of the Longways dance than of the dance in any of its earlier forms.

XVIII. CENTURY.

The beginning of the 18th century was a critical moment in the history of the social dance of Europe. During the last half-century, with the efforts to discover a scientific technique, the dances grew steadily more conventional and the style more stilted and affected. It is obvious that this tendency, if allowed to continue unchecked, was bound sooner or later to lead to a reaction and a refusal on the part of the dancers any longer to practise a form of dance from which they derived no enjoyment. The pursuit of pleasure, worthy or unworthy, is after all the primary aim of the dancer and, if the dances with which society provides him fail to satisfy this elementary requirement, he will seek elsewhere for his gratification. This was the position in 1700, history thus repeating itself and reproducing the situation which had occurred 150 years before in Arbeau's lifetime. Then, it will be remembered, the Basse Dance was quietly dismissed and replaced in France by a type of dance quasi-folk in character and mostly native in origin. This remedy was now repeated; the Court dances were gradually jettisoned, and a substitute found to some extent in the English Country Dances in the toned down and modified form which they had now acquired.

During the latter years of the 17th century our Country Dances had begun to find their way to the Continent. According to Macaulay, the Duke of Monmouth, when at the Hague in 1685, "had taught the English Country Dances to the Dutch ladies." The earliest authenticated evidence is, however, the first collection of our dances to be published abroad, the *Recueil de Contredanses* (Paris, 1706), compiled by Feuillet. This contained the description, in the new choreography, of 32 Longways dances, 16 of which can be traced to the 10th edition of Playford's *Dancing-Master* (1698), the remainder being composed "after the English model" by the editor and his friends. Although "Madame la Dauphine," Feuillet tells us in his preface, had previously introduced the Country Dances into France, it was no doubt this collection that first brought them to the notice of

24

the general public and led to the great popularity which they enjoyed during the Regency (1715-23). By 1723 Jacques Bonnet could write in his *Histoire Générale de la Danse* that ever since the wedding of the Duc de Bourgogne he had watched with regret the gradual disappearance, year by year, of the ancient serious and dignified dances that had been danced at Court from time immemorial; that it had been only with difficulty that the Branle, Courante and Minuet had been preserved, for the young men of the Court had already ousted them for the contredanses which, he regretted, had none of the dignity and distinction which characterised the older dances. Our Country Dance quickly penetrated into Spain as the *contra-danza*, and into Germany as the *contretanz*. They were established in Austria before 1717, when Lady Mary Wortley Montagu wrote from Vienna that "the ball always concludes with English Country Dances to the number of 30 or 40 couples, and so ill danced that there is very little pleasure in them"; while Walpole wrote from Italy in 1749, "they are fond to a degree of our Country Dances."

Hitherto, fashionable England had looked to France for its clothes, manners, etiquette and dances, and people soon refused to believe that the tide had turned and that we had now sent dances to France instead of importing them. Seizing upon the resemblance between the English and French names of the dance, they boldly proclaimed that the dance was French, not English, in origin. *The Gentleman's Magazine* (1758) put the matter concisely, thus: "As our dances in general come from France, so does the country-dance, which is a manifest corruption of the French *contre-danse*, where a number of people placing themselves *opposite* to one another begin a figure." Since even now this notion persists, and in many of our dictionaries and histories the origin of the Country Dance is attributed to France, it may be as well to assemble the governing facts.

Weaver, the English historian of the Dance, was under no misapprehension with regard to its origin, for he wrote of the Country Dance as "the peculiar Growth of this Nation" (1712); nor was Feuillet, for he distinctly states in the Preface to his Collection that "Les Anglois en sont les premiers inventeurs." This was corroborated by Jacques Bonnet (1723), who says that he had been told that the contredanse had been introduced into France by an English dancing-master some 12 or 15 years before.

How and when the word *contredanse* got into the French language it is important to know. The only recorded instance of its use in France before the 18th century is in the diary of Maréchal de Bassompierre, the French plenipotentiary at our Court in 1626: "Nov. 15, 1626. Et en suite nous nous mismes à danser des contredanses, jusques a quatre heures après minuict." What he here calls contredanses were of course our Country Dances; they could not have been anything else.

The word, however, could not have been in general use at that time for it is not in the Geneva edition of Richelet's *Dictionnaire François* (1690), nor in that of 1710, but is included in the Amsterdam edition of 1722; nor is it to be found in the *Dictionnaire* of Furetière (1690); nor again in the first edition of the *Dictionnaire de l'Académie* (1694), though it does appear in the later edition of 1718.

Except, therefore, in Bassompierre's Diary the word does not appear to occur in French literature before 1706, when Feuillet published his Collection. Nevertheless, it is certainly difficult to explain how Bassompierre came to translate "Country Dance" into "contredanse." It may have been as a phonetic equivalent, like *bifteck*, or merely a literal translation, *contrée-danse*. It is just possible that Feuillet used *contredanse* in the sense given in the *Gentleman's Magazine*, because the only form of the Country Dance that he knew, or at any rate included in his book, was the Longways, where *contre* (opposite) would have some meaning. But Bassompierre would not have used it for this reason because the typical dances of 1625, which he, of course, would have seen, were Rounds, Square-eights, etc., where *contre* in the sense of "opposite" would be meaningless.

Further confusion was caused when some years later, about 1740, the French used the word to describe an entirely different dance, a Square dance for four couples, which later on they re-named the Quadrille. Some writers, Chappell for instance, have argued that this French square-dance was but a Gallic version of our own Country Dance Square-eight. But there is not a particle of evidence that the Country Dance in this form, or indeed in any form other than the Longways, was ever used or known in France. Moreover, an examination of these dances as described by La Cuisse (1760-4) shows that they had little in common with our English Square-eight. What, I believe, happened was that the French, inspired by our example, took a leaf out of our book and made a drawing-room dance out of one of their own folk-dances (probably the Cotillon), and this, not perhaps unnaturally, they also called a contredanse, using that term in a generic sense. If they had called it Quadrille in the first instance no confusion between this dance and the Longways contredanse would have arisen, nor would the English origin of the latter have been disputed.

The facts then are these: (1), that since 1650 the word Country Dance has been used in England as the generic title of our national dance in its various formations, Rounds, Square-eights, Longways, etc.; (2), that before the 18th century the word contredanse occurs but once in French literature, when it was used as the French equivalent of the English Country Dance; (3), that the word did not come into general use in France until 1706, in which year Feuillet published his collection of Longways dances under that designation; (4), that during the first 30 or 40 years of the 18th century the word was used in France exclusively to denote our Country Dance in its Longways formation; and (5), that subsequently it came to be applied in France to a Square-dance founded upon the Cotillon, or some other French folk-dance, which in the latter years of the century came to be called the Quadrille.

It appears, then, that we not only supplied Europe in the first instance with a new dance, a modified folk-dance, to take the place of the discredited Court dances, but we inspired other nations to follow our example and to make use of their own folk-dances as we had done with ours. This is what the French apparently did, and what I suspect the Danes and Swedes must also have done, judging by the number of contredanses included in their folk-dance Collections. If I am right, then all these three nations used the term contredanse in very much the same sense as Branle was used in the 16th century.

The Italians, after assimilating the contredanse in both its forms, the English Longways and the French Square-dance (which they distinguished by the terms *indeterminata and determinata, i.e.*, dances in which an indeterminate or a fixed number of dancers took part), also converted into social dances the Tarantella, Furlano and other folk-dances of their own. The Germans again, who distinguished the English and French forms of the *Contratanz* by calling the former the English and the latter the French dances, also followed the French lead and admitted many of their peasant dances, including the Ländler, the prototype of the Waltz, into their dancing halls.

The Cotillon, the French folk-dance (*cotte* was the short petticoat worn by peasants) and the forerunner of the Quadrille, which had been introduced into the salons of France earlier in the century, was brought to England about 1770 (Plates 50 & 53). It at once won favour here, and from 1780 publishers included New Cotillons in their annual publications of New Country Dances. Also and at about the same period, Ecossoises and an English adaptation of the Scottish Reel for three to six dancers were danced side by side with the Country Dances. The Ecossoises were very similar to the English Country Dances but executed more energetically, to a faster *tempo*, and often to Scottish tunes.

The ceremonial observed at the Court balls in France in the 18th century was very much the same as it had been in the 17th. Rameau, in his *Maître à Danser* (1725), describes the procedure in detail. When every one had been placed in Order, according to Rank; the Lords on the left Side, and the Ladies on the Right; and they had made their Honours, the King and his Partner led up the Brawl, all the Lords and Ladies following. "When," in the words of Essex's translation (1728), "at the End of the Strain the King and Queen went to the Bottom, the next Couple led up the Brawl in their Turn, and so successively till their Majesties came at the Top again." After the Brawl they danced the Gavotte in the same Order and then double Dances. By his time,

27

Rameau says, the Minuet had replaced the Courante after the Branle. It is consequently not easy to understand how he regarded the Gavotte.

In England even at the end of the 18th century the Ball sometimes opened with a Promenade round the room in couples to a marching tune—the survival, no doubt, of the Brawl. Then Minuets were danced —at Bath Beau Nash always led the first. Thereafter none but Country Dances were danced. When the first was announced the couples stood up in numerical order—each lady having received a card with a number which she had to pin conspicuously on her dress—and were arranged by the Master of the Ceremonies in sets of nine. The leading lady of the first Set had the "call" or privilege of setting the figures and choosing the tune, which was played once before the dance began. The dance continued until the leading couple had returned to their original positions at the head of the column and, in addition, had moved down three places. At the conclusion of the dance the executants remained in their places, the couple now at the top having the Call for the next dance.

This century, then, witnessed the decline of all the old Court dances, with the exception of the Minuet and the Gavotte, and the installation at first of the English Country Dance and afterwards of other folk-dances in their stead. True, it was a somewhat formal and sophisticated Country Dance that we exported to Europe, very different from the merry dance with which Queen Elizabeth was so "exceedingly pleased"; yet it managed to retain, even in the days of knee-breeches, swords and snuff-boxes, of voluminous skirts and mountainous head-dresses, what a contemporary "lady of distinction" aptly called its "gay simplicity," the peculiar gift of the people of whose genius it was the expression. It is pleasant to remember that our Continental neigh-bours of that time were dancing with enjoyment, though not perhaps exactly in our English way, our Greensleeves, Christchurch Bells, Joan's Placket and Buttered Pease, even though disguised under such strange titles as Les Manches Vertes, Les Carillons d'Oxfort, Jeanne qui saute, and Pizelli al Burro.

XIX. CENTURY.

During the first quarter of the 19th century the Country Dance fully upheld its pre-eminence in the ball-rooms of England, although the two foreign dances which were destined eventually to dethrone it were both introduced during this period—the Waltz in 1812, and the Quadrille four years later.

Curiously enough, the Country Dance was never more popular than in the years immediately preceding its decline, and it was in this period—1810-25—that were published the best and most complete technical books on the dance in its eighteenth-century form, written by

28

ENGLAND. XVIII. CENTURY.

T. ROWLANDSON.   BALL AT THE ASSEMBLY ROOMS, BATH.   (ENGRAVED 1798).
WATER-COLOUR.   (In the Collection of Brig.-General Noel M. Lake, C.B.).

PLATE 2.

Thomas Wilson, "Dancing-Master from the King's Theatre Opera House." These books fully reflect the remarkable revival of interest in dancing, almost amounting to a mania, which followed the close of the Napoleonic wars. It became the most popular and fashionable amusement, and was pursued with ardour by all classes of the kingdom. Teachers of dancing were in high demand and drove a roaring trade; public balls were crowded out and, wherever suitable accommodation could be found, dancing rooms were opened to which admission was free, with or without invitation, the proprietors, usually dance-professors, relying for their remuneration upon the deposit "of a piece of money of not less value than sixpence for the care of hats and bonnets." Even "Apprentices and Servants are frequently invited," Wilson adds somewhat scornfully.

History records other instances of an unrestrained indulgence in dancing after wars or great political disturbances. In France, for instance, after the Revolution and almost before the Terror was over, 1,800 dancing salons were opened every evening in Paris. After the Civil War in America, too, there was a like popular craze; while, to come down to our own time, the rage for dancing which set in immediately after the Armistice has not yet abated.

The genesis of the Waltz has been the subject of much controversy. The French have claimed it as the direct descendant of the 16th century Volta, unmindful of the facts that the two dances have few points of resemblance, and that the Volta fell into disuse soon after the close of the 16th century and had not been danced in France for at least 150 years. The Waltz first appeared in Bavaria and Austria about 1780, and there is little doubt but that it was a drawing-room adaptation of the Ländler which is still danced by the peasantry in the villages of Southern Germany, to the same slow rhythm of the charming and delicate tunes which Beethoven and Schubert wrote for them. The Waltz had therefore served a full twenty years' apprenticeship in France and Germany before it reached our shores, and it came to us therefore in a highly polished form. It was at first danced in several different ways. There was the German Waltz and the French Waltz, the latter in three forms called by Wilson the Slow, the Sauteuse, and the Jetté or Quick Sauteuse Waltz. These three varieties differed in *tempi*, in the positions of the arms and hands, and to some extent in the steps also, and were usually danced one after the other without pause.

Although the dance did not reach us until 1812, numerous Collections of Waltz-airs had been published in England for twenty years or more before that date and used as Country Dance Tunes, furnished with Country Dance figures and called Waltz Country Dances. This ready acceptance of the tunes of the Waltz was not, however, extended to the dance itself. The position in which partners were required to engage in the new dance shocked the national sense of propriety and was deemed grossly indecorous. "No event," it was said, "ever produced so great a sensation in English society. Mothers forbade it, and every ball-room became a scene of feud and contention." Byron—and he was no prude— satirised it in scathing terms in *The Waltz, An Apostrophic Hymn*, 1812, under the pseudonym of Horace Hornem, Esq. We who live in a less fastidious age can afford to smile at the storm of indignation which the Waltz aroused, more especially when we recall the quite seemly and wholly inoffensive positions (Plate 65) against which this outburst was directed. Remembering, however, that the Country Dancers at that time indulged in nothing more daringly intimate than the taking of hands, we need not be surprised that the more familiar embrace in the Waltz should have seemed a little improper. The opposition to the dance was very general, and quite sincere, and it was many years before the Waltz gained a sure foothold in the ball-rooms of the metropolis, and still longer before it was universally accepted in the provinces.

The Quadrille was formally introduced into English society by Lady Jersey and her friends at Almack's in 1816. Originally the figures were put together by the dancers themselves, a practice with which Country Dancers were quite familiar. Wilson's *Treatise on Quadrille Dancing* (1818) contains the description of 50 different movements, with instructions how to combine them into figures, many of these movements being Cotillon figures already familiar to English dancers. New figures were often composed by dancing masters and published with appropriate music. One of the most popular publications was Payne's *Six Sets of Quadrilles* (1820), the first of which was a set that had achieved so great a popularity in Paris at the end of the 18th century that it had in large measure superseded all others. This was the Set which Lady Jersey introduced at Almack's and which ultimately became the only form in which the Quadrille was danced in England. Its figures were named Le Pantalon, L'Eté, La Poule, La Pastourelle (or alternatively, La Trénise), and a Finale.

The Lancers, "A Second Set of Quadrilles with entirely new Figures, as danced by the Nobility and Gentry of Tenby in the Summer of 1819," was compiled by Joseph Hart and published in London in 1820. This also contained five figures, La Rose, La Lodaiska, La Dorset, Les Lanciers and L'Etoile. The tunes of Quadrille figures were only rarely original; they were usually arrangements, or adaptations, of operatic or popular airs of the day. The tune to the third figure of the Lancers, La Dorset, for example, was Poor Robin's Maggot from Playford's *Dancing-Master*, which was also used in *The Beggar's Opera* and sung to the words "If the heart of a Man."

The Quadrille, unlike the Waltz, quickly achieved favour in England and, together with the Lancers, won a place in our drawing-rooms of which they have only recently been dispossessed. In the

30

form in which we received it from France the dance depended for its effect quite as much upon its elaborate steps as upon its figures. When, subsequently, these decorative steps and graces were discarded and the dancers merely walked through the figures, the dance was robbed of its chief claim to recognition, and it is a little difficult to account for the popularity it continued so long afterwards to enjoy. Probably even in its debased form it fulfilled, however inadequately, the function of a ceremonial drawing-room dance, as couple-dances like the Waltz could not.

As the popularity of the Quadrille and Waltz increased that of the Country Dance waned, and when the Polka, a Bohemian dance introduced in 1845, and subsequently the Schottische, the Mazurka, the Barn Dance, and other couple-dances also competed with it, it was finally deposed from the predominant position which it had held in England for nearly two centuries. Nevertheless, although exiled from the drawing-room, the practice of country dancing has never been entirely discontinued. Sir Roger is still sometimes used as a " finishing-dance " at children's parties, while in country places the dance still lingers, usually in the Progressive Longways form, though in the northern counties a few of the older types still survive.

XX. CENTURY.

During the latter years of the last century and the early years of the present the Quadrille and Waltz in their turn were fast losing favour ; they had run their course, were worn out, and the time had come for a change. Hitherto, European dancers had looked to their own folk-dances for fresh material ; now, and for the first time, their eyes were turned to America. The first dance to challenge the Waltz was the Turkey-trot, now known as the One-Step, hailing from San Francisco ; then came a South American dance, the Argentine Tango, first to Paris and later to England, but this, owing to its executive difficulties and the bizarre, theatrical character of some of its movements never succeeded in establishing itself in Europe, although it left its mark on subsequent developments. The Boston-Waltz was the third dance, also from the American Continent, and this together with the One-Step and the Tango are the basic forms from which the many varieties of the present-day drawing-room dances have been derived—this, at any rate, is the theory advanced by the Misses Kinny (*The Dance;* New York, 1914), whose opinion should be authoritative.

These dances, popularly and collectively known as the Jazz, came to us heavily charged with negroid characteristics, presumably contracted in the Southern States of North America, and associated with a very distinctive type of syncopated, or rag-time, music. The

31

sawing movements of the arms, the restless, vibratory shakings of the shoulders and the close embrace, the merciless tom-tom rhythm and clatter of the music, all of which may be traced to negro influence, have since been considerably modified, and dancers now affect a far more restrained and dignified style than that which characterised the dance in its earlier form. Had it not been for the unsettlement of mind, manners and habits, which followed in the train of the Great War, and the fact that at the moment this was the only available dance with which to satisfy the craze for dancing, which set in after the Armistice, it is permissible to doubt whether a dance of so inferior, and in its earlier forms so objectionable, a type, would have gained a foothold in this country. Truth to tell, there is but little to be advanced in its favour and much that can be charged against it. Looking back over the long series of social dances, from the fourteenth-century Basse-dances to the nineteenth-century Waltzs and Quadrilles, one can but marvel what the Jazz has to do in such company. It is, moreover, the only dance of the series associated with music other than of the first order.

The Jazz brings us down to our own times, but the survey would be incomplete were it to ignore the remarkable revival of folk-dancing which has taken place during the last twenty years or more in this country, Scandinavia and, more recently and to a lesser extent, in Germany. The purpose of the revival is not to extract in a piecemeal fashion from the store of dances created and accumulated by the folk one or more choice specimens to serve in the drawing-room, but to explore the folk-dance repertory in its entirety, every species of every type, the ritual Sword and Morris dances no less than the social Country Dances, and, so far from endeavouring to adapt or "improve" them, to insist that they shall, in the first instance at any rate, be presented and assimilated in their purest and most unsullied forms. The variety, the artistic wealth, the beauty of the dances and their tunes, and the high technical development that many of them display, have come as a revelation to the present generation. If the movement succeeds in disseminating an accurate knowledge of the technique of the folk-dance and in arousing a widespread appreciation of its artistic worth, it may lead to creative results of permanent value, initiating, perhaps, a genuine development of the art of the dance which previous efforts have failed to achieve. It is significant, too, that, in the matter of the Country Dance, present taste has fastened upon the seventeenth-century dances preserved in the earlier editions of *The Dancing-Master*, because, if progress is to be made, this, the moment when the dance was at the apex of its development, must necessarily be the point of departure. Whether this revival is to lead to the results above foreshadowed, or to prove sterile, lies in the womb of the future; but this at any rate may be said of it that it is an experiment of a sort that has not before, in the history of the dance, been seriously undertaken.

32

SPECTACULAR DANCE.

SPECTACULAR DANCE.

Up to this point our investigation has been confined to the consideration of the dance in its purest and most absolute form, in which it rested for its expression solely upon its own instinctive and peculiar methods, unaided by any art other than that of music from which, in the nature of things, it can never be divorced. But throughout the whole of its history dancing has also been used in combination and partnership with other arts, as one of the elements of a composite form of entertainment known variously as mummings, disguisings, revels, masquerades, or masques and, ultimately, as the ballet, or *ballet d'action*. Arbeau in his *Orchésographie* frequently accounts for certain attributes of the dance which he is describing by saying that it had been used in a masquerade, by which he means a primitive form of dance-drama or pantomime. Diversions of this nature, consisting of dancing, verse spoken and sung, miming and dramatic action, together with elaborate costumes and scenic accessories, had long been common in various countries, more particularly in Italy.

These diversions were for the most part derived from traditional folk-customs, many of them quasi-religious rituals dating from pagan times, such as the Florentine Trionfi and Canti. They might be bands of men parading the streets at carnival times, disguised in grotesque masks, smeared with soot or flour, sometimes dressed as women, singing Carnival songs; or processions of wheeled cars containing antique momeries or allegorical characters accompanied by men, masked and disguised, chanting their praises; or again, groups of singers, musicians and dancers with torch-bearers, who would burst uninvited into balls and assemblies, entertain their hosts with dances and songs, and play dice and dance with them. In the fifteenth and sixteenth centuries these had crystalized into two forms, mascarades and intermedi. The former, when played in large open spaces, consisted of processions of decorated cars, cavalcades lavishly caparisoned, tourneys, etc.; or, when presented indoors, of a series of songs, recitations and dances, loosely strung together with sometimes a presenter to explain their

Fig. (f) Fools' Dance from the manuscript of the Alexander. Romance (14th cent.) in the Bodleian Library.

35

purpose in song or speech.   The intermedi were groups of songs, dances, cortèges, etc., interposed between the acts of a play, the action of which they interrupted rather than aided, or between the courses of a banquet, as in the celebrated Banquet-ballet performed at the festivities organised by Bergonzio di Botta at the nuptials of Galeazzo, Duke of Milan, and Isabella of Aragon (1489).

The dances in the mascarades and intermedi were of four kinds, Danses figurées, Balli or Balletti, Brandi, and Moresques.   The Danses Figurées consisted of a succession of tableaux in which the dancers were grouped in various geometrical patterns, sometimes mounted on horses (Plate 37).   The figures, many of which are described by Father Ménétrier (*Des Ballets anciens et modernes*, 1682), were frankly spectacular rather than expressive and of the nature of pageantry rather than of dancing, and are not to be confounded with what is ordinarily meant by figure-dancing, *i.e.*, the weaving of patterns by dancers in motion, as in the Country Dance.   Bacon had no doubt the Danses Figurées in mind when he characterized " turning dances into figure " a " childish curiosity " (Plate 29).

Balli and balletti were the ordinary social dances of the day.

Brandi were costumed theatrical dances of an expressive and dramatic character devised by choreographers.

The term Moresque was used in a wide and somewhat indefinite sense.   It included the traditional Morris Dance, but was more often applied to any grotesque dance that was improvised (not pre-arranged like the brandi) and performed by dancers who were masked and disguised in bizarre costume, representing savages, animals, monkeys, etc. (Plate 17).

Spectacular diversions of a like kind based upon folk rituals were common elsewhere than in Italy.   The earliest mention of one in England was a visit paid to Richard II. in 1377 by 130 citizens of London disguised with vizards and accompanied by musicians and torch-bearers, who invited their hosts to dice, then danced and drank with them and departed.   The dancing of the visitors with the spectators— " commoning," as it was called—disappeared in England in the course of the next century, the masquers dancing with one another only ; but in the early years of the 16th century it was re-introduced from Italy where the custom had survived.   The commoning thenceforth remained an essential element of the " disguising " or " masque," as at the close of Henry VIII.'s reign this form of entertainment came to be called.

The developments which took place in Italy during the fifteenth and sixteenth centuries were summed up in the Ballet Comique de la Reine," performed in Paris at the Court of Henri III. and Catherine de' Medici in 1581, during the wedding festivities of the Duc de Joyeuse and Marguerite of Lorraine, sister of the Queen of France (Plate 25).

36

The book was written and the ballet produced by an Italian, Baltazarini, called Beaujoyeulx, valet-de-chambre to Catherine. The importance of this production in the history and development of opera and ballet is very great. Not that it contained any material that had not previously been used in the mascarades and intermedi, but because of the deft way in which the various elements, songs, dances, recitations, processions, were welded together for the development of the subject which was the tale of Circe. The ballet fully justified the claim set forth by its author in his introduction :—" J'ay animé et fait parler le Ballet, et chanter et resonner la Comédie : et y adjuistant plusieurs rares et riches representations et ornements je puis dire avoir contenté en un corps bien proportionné l'œuil, l'oreille et l'entendement." The ballet displays the influence upon Beaujoyeulx of the humanists and their theatrical theories.

Owing to religious disturbances and depletion of the royal purse, ballets on a large scale were discontinued in France, and this led to a reversion at first to an early form of mascarade, and in the latter years of the century to a combination of this with the ballet-dramatique—known as the ballet-mascarade. In the first years of the seventeenth century chanted recitatives displaced spoken dialogues, and the ballet-mascarade became known as the ballet-mélodramatique. This movement in the direction of opera continued, and by the third decade of the seventeenth century the ballet-à-entrées made its appearance, in which the dances were treated as episodes more or less divorced from the main action of the drama. During this period, that is from 1581, the date of the production of the Ballet Comique, to 1650, a development on similar lines took place in Italy with an added emphasis on the spectacular side and on that of mélodrame or opera (Plates 28, 35 & 36).

In England the artistic theories embodied in the Ballet Comique were frankly accepted and made the starting point for further developments. There were only two directions, as Mr. E. K. Chambers points out, in which improvements could be made—the concentration of the scenery and the addition of the anti-masque. For the first of these Inigo Jones, who had served his apprenticeship in Italy, was chiefly responsible, and for the second Ben Jonson. It must be understood that the masque in England, as in France and Italy, was performed by amateurs and aristocrats—even the King and Queen taking part in France—although the general public was sometimes admitted to the performances. Despite, too, the high literary value of the books, especially those by Ben Jonson, Campion and others, the dancing was the chief and most popular feature of the masque; scenery, dialogue and songs were merely accessory to the dancing, which occupied in its performance the major part of the time allotted to the entertainment. So popular was the dancing that the spectators—including, it is said, James I. himself—were apt to show impatience if the introductory speech was unduly prolonged, and this led to the substitution of a preliminary dance, known as the anti-masque, for the spoken prologue.

The anti-masque was so named because it was a foil or false masque, *i.e.*, antithetic in character to the masque proper which succeeded it. If, for instance, the entry dance was to be the apotheosis of beauty the anti-masque which preceded it would be " a revel in the ugly and horrible." The anti-masque was therefore usually a grotesque dance " full of pre-posterous change and gesticulation," in which the dancers did " all things contrary to the custom of men, dancing back to back and hip to hip .   .   . and making their circles backward to the left hand, with strange fantastic motions of their heads and bodies." Bacon describes them as " Fooles, Satyres, Baboones, Wild men, Antiques, and Beastes," on which account the anti-masque was sometimes called the antic-masque.   These grotesque anti-masques (Plates 33 & 34) were performed by professional dancers from the theatres, where some of them were afterwards used as interludes. The Satyrs' dance in " A Winter's Tale " was originally an anti-masque dance.

By the beginning of the seventeenth century the form of the English masque had become more or less stereotyped in so far as the dance-entries were concerned. The amateur dancers, or masquers, varied in their number, but it was usually 8, 12 or 16. They gave three formal dances, called respectively the Entry, the Main and the Going-out dance. These were danced on a platform erected on the floor of the room, and from it the dancers descended after their second dance, the Main, for the commoning or " revels."

There were, then, three different kinds of dance in the masque— the " intermixed " dances performed with the spectators in the revels; the masquers " own " dances in the three formal entries; and the anti-masque dances, corresponding to the Balletti, the Danses Figurées and Brandi, and the Moresques of Italy. The first of these, the intermixed dances, were naturally the social dances of the day, usually galliards, corantos and lavoltas, more rarely brawls and morascos, or moresques.

The masquers' own dances were specially devised by professional dancing-masters and carefully rehearsed for the occasion. Some of these were Danses Figurées, derived from Italy, as, for instance, that in Jonson's *Masque of Queens* (1609), in which the performers were disposed in the form of letters spelling the name of Charles, the Duke of York. It is more probable, however, that the normal masquers' dance was a variation or development of the dances of the day, which would be far more easily learned by the amateurs and technically more nearly within their range. What evidence there is seems to support this view.   There is, for instance, the " Grayes Inn Maske," or 'Mad Tom," printed in *The English Dancing Master* (1650), complete with tunes and movements. There are two separate airs, the first in even measure, the second in triple, and the dance, which is arranged for four

38

couples in column, consists of figures and movements with which every Country Dancer of that day would be familiar. Of the 75 masque dance-tunes of this period that I have examined nearly all, excluding the anti-masque tunes, are in form similar to that of the Grayes Inn Maske. It is possible that some of the dances in *The English Dancing-Master* were originally masque dances, but there is only one dance in that volume, The New Figary, with a double-tune like that of the Grayes Inn Maske. The name of the dancing-master who designed the dances in the masque *Oberon* (1611) was Confess, and it may be that the dance with his name as its title printed in the first edition of Playford's book was one that he composed for that production. It would not be safe to generalise from a single instance, but to develop and elaborate their own dances for the purpose of the Masque was the most natural and reasonable thing to do. Moreover, as we shall see later, this is what actually was done in the Opera-ballets of the seventeenth and eighteenth centuries.

We have little information concerning the anti-masque dances beyond the fact that they were grotesque and performed by dancers from the theatres. The only dance mentioned in this connection is the Morris, a term which at that time, as we have seen, had a wide signification and included other dances as well as the traditional folk-dance. The theatrical companies of those days included men competent to give musical performances, to dance and even to give acrobatic displays, and these were responsible for the dances and songs which it was customary to give in the interludes and at the conclusion of the play. The "afterpiece" was usually a Jig, a term which at first meant merely a dance, but later on comprehended a short, farcical sketch for two or three characters with much dancing and singing. What the nature of the dancing was we can only guess, but it was certainly very lively, often grotesque, and may have included vaulting and other acrobatic tricks. It should be added that the anti-masque dance-airs were faster in tempo and more irregular in form and rhythm than those of the masquers' own dances.

The masque declined in the middle of the seventeenth century, and its re-appearance after the Restoration was in the theatre, not at Court, and as opera, not masque—the Purcell opera. This revival, however, was short-lived and came to an end with the death of Purcell. The eighteenth-century operas of this country, with the exception of the ballad-operas, were either foreign importations or, if written in England by Handel and others, cast in the foreign mould.

With the accession of Louis XIV. to the throne the lead in the development of the ballet passed to France, where it remained to the close of the following century. Louis XIV. was, as we have seen, an inveterate dancer and a notable patron of the art in every form. In 1651, at the age of 13, he danced in *Cassandra*, and continued to appear in a succession of ballets, including some of the comédie-ballets of Molière, until he retired in 1669 at the age of 30. The king, of course, ordinarily played leading and reputable parts only, such as Apollo or Jupiter, while the less exalted characters were impersonated by members of his Court. Later they were assisted by a certain number of professional women dancers known as "femmes pantomimes."

In 1661 Louis gave further proof of his interest in the dance by founding the Royal Academy of Dancing, in order to counteract "a great number of abuses which have been introduced during the disorder of the last wars into the said art." "Many ignorant people," the preamble continues, "have tried to disfigure the dance, the majority being people of quality, so that we see few among those of our Court and Suite who would be able to take part in our ballets."

This was certainly severe upon the dancers of his Court, but Louis rightly perceived that the lack of competent executants was at that time the greatest obstacle to the development of spectacular dancing. The training of professional dancers at the Royal Academy soon began to have its effect, and it was not long before the ballets, hitherto exclusively the pastime of the Court, were produced in the theatres. In 1669 the privilege of producing opera or musical representations in the French theatres and in the French tongue was granted to Perrin and Cambert. Two years later, in 1671, *Pomone*, the first ballet described as an opera-ballet, was produced in the public theatre, that of the Rue Mazarin. The book was by Perrin, the proprietor of the theatre, the music by Cambert (afterwards attached to the Court of Charles II. in London, where he died in 1677), and the dances by Beauchamps. It drew crowded houses for eight months. Lully followed suit with the *Fêtes de Bacchus et de l'Amour* at the Bel Air Theatre in 1672. In the same year Louis reconstructed his academy, and in letters patent authorised "our faithful, well-beloved Jean-Baptiste Lully to add to the Royal Academy of Music and Dancing a School suitable to educate pupils as much for dancing as for singing."

During the next few years the ballet gradually passed from the Court to the theatre, until at the death of Louis XIV. (1715) the Court-ballet ceased, and the transference was complete. For some while, however, the theatre had still partly to depend upon the Court for its dancers. Hitherto, it had not been the custom for women-performers to appear on the French stage, except of course at Court, but Lully impressed by his experiences of the Court-ballet ignored this tradition, and in 1681 produced *le Triomphe de l'Amour*, in which for the first time on the public stage female parts were impersonated by professional *danseuses* from the Royal Academy, of whom Mlle. Lafontaine was the chief. Liberated from this restriction and now firmly established in the theatre, the ballet was free to develop unhampered. The Abbé Du Bos describes in 1719 how music and the dance (especially that of

40

Fig. (g)   Costume of a Ballerina, c. 1700.   From a print.

the theatre) had vied with each other in increasing their swiftness and
characterization since the time, 80 years before, when the ballet dance
scarcely differed from that of the ordinary ball.   Action, too, had
increased, and women had followed men.   Their progress was, however, doubtless retarded by the heavy, cumbersome dresses which
ballerinas had inherited from the Court ladies.   They wore high-heeled
shoes, heavy skirts puffed out with paniers and reaching to the ground,
towering wigs, sometimes three feet in height, decked with ribbons,
flowers and plumes, and they covered their faces with masks.   They
carried a leopard's skin, if a Bacchante; a wreath of flowers, if Flora;
a bow and arrows, if Cupid; a pair of bellows, if Zephyrus.   Thus
equipped, it is obvious that women were incapable of performing
anything more violent than the gliding, deliberate and stately steps of
the Court dances of the day.   An examination of Lully's scores shows
that the dances in the entrées (though not specifically so named) were
gavottes, minuets, chaconnes, bourées, gigues, and canaries.   Campra
(1660-1744) added to these loures, rigaudons, passepieds, sarabandes,

41

musettes, etc. Although his ballet-music shows a considerable advance upon that of his predecessors, Rameau in this respect adhered to tradition and made use of the ancient measures, even though he often treated them fugually and contrapuntally.

An attempt to increase the range of steps in the ballet is associated with the name of Camargo (1710-1770), who made her début in Paris in 1726 and retired from the stage in 1741 (Plate 43). In 1730 she is said to have introduced an entrechat of four cuts or crosses, and later in her career the saut de basque, jetés, battus en l'air, etc. (*Nécrologe des Hommes célèbres de France*, Paris 1770). To obtain the necessary liberty of movement which these steps demanded Camargo discarded the high-heeled shoe in favour of the ballet-slipper, shortened her skirt to a point midway between knee and ankle, and added an under-garment which the execution of her steps *en haut* necessitated. To credit her, as many writers have done, with the invention of the entrechat is unwarranted. They were known many years before her time. "Entrechats or cross-capers of three, four and six crossings" are included in Feuillet's *Chorégraphie* (1701); while something closely akin is shown in the plate of a Florentine masque of 1637 (Plate 35), and perhaps corresponds to the *Capriola intrecciata* described by Caroso (1581). A similar error is often made in assigning the invention of the pirouette to Mlle. Heinel in 1766, for this step is mentioned by Ménétrier (1682) and described by Feuillet and Rameau (1725). There can be little doubt but that many steps of this character were known and practised by men long before women and by jig and extemporary dancers such as those of the Commedia dell' Arte before they found their way into the ballet, though, indeed, his exertions in parodying one of Beauchamps' entrées were said to have caused the death, in 1688, of Dominique, the famous Harlequin. Of Beauchamps, La Bruyère wrote in 1680: "Would the dancer Cobus please you, who, throwing up his feet in front, turns once in the air before regaining the floor?" And again, speaking of Pécour (who made his début in 1687): "Where will you find a young man who leaps higher into the air whilst dancing or who cuts better capers?"

The only indication known to me of the manner in which ballet-steps were used in the Court dances is the choreography by Gaetan Vestris of a gavotte (printed by Zorn in his *Grammar of the Art of Dancing*, 1885), and this includes *entrechats à quatre ou huit, pirouettes battues* of two or more turns, *ailes de pigeon*, etc.

The chief dancers of this period were Beauchamps, Pécour (who succeeded Beauchamp on the death of Lully in 1687), Lestang, Dupré (known as le Grand), Blondy (nephew of Beauchamps), Ballon, Dumoulin and Marcel (singer as well as dancer). Of the women-dancers the most distinguished were Lafontaine, Guyot, Prévost (Camargo's first teacher) and Sallé. Noverre, in his *Lettres sur la*

42

danse (1760), paid tribute " to the elegance of Mlle. Prévost's dancing of the passepied; to the voluptuous grace with which Mlle. Sallé and M. Dumoulin invested the musette; to Mlle. Camargo for the way in which she excelled in the tambourin; and to Dupré for the distinction he imparted to the chaconne and passecaille." Several of these dancers are eulogised by Rameau in the introduction to his *Maître à Danser*.

The reform initiated by Camargo was carried a step further by Mlle. Sallé, who appeared in London in the opera Pygmalion (1734) clad in a gauze tunic "sans panier, sans jupes, sans corps, échevelée et sans aucun ornement sur la tête " (*Le Mercure de France*). She was not, however, permitted to dance at the opera in Paris in this scanty attire.

For a greater reformer dancers had to wait for another thirty years until the advent of Jean Georges Noverre (1727-1810), who was to make a valiant attempt to sweep away the ridiculous dresses, the masks, the mechanical rules of step-combinations, the stereotyped mythological and allegorical plots, the hard and fast sequence of dance-entries and other disabilities which were inherited from the Ballet de Cour. Noverre was a very remarkable man, of much cultivation, a fine dancer (pupil of Dupré), a great teacher, and a composer of imagination. His views concerning the dance and the place which the ideal ballet, as he conceived it, should occupy, were set forth in his *Lettres sur la danse et sur les ballets* (1760), and later on in his *Lettres sur les Arts imitateurs en général et sur la danse en particulier* (1807). Finding Paris too conservative and unsympathetic, he retired first to Lyons and afterwards to Stuttgart, where he held the office of Maître à Ballet. Here for ten years, together with Gaetan Vestris and Dauberval, he steadily worked out his theories and sought to put them into practice. In 1775 he composed and produced *Médée et Jason* (Plate 57), which he called, without qualification, a ballet. By this he meant a dance-pantomime, in which narrative and dramatic action were portrayed solely by dancing and miming without the aid of singing or verbal explanation.

The art of miming had long been practised in Italy either as an unbroken tradition from Roman days or, according to another view, as a spontaneous growth of the fifteenth century. The Commedia dell'Arte had been played by Italians in France from 1640 onwards, while Italian comedies were performed in Paris in the early years of the eighteenth century. Noverre, however, was the first to make miming an integral factor of the ballet and thus to establish the ballet d'action. He acquired much of his knowledge concerning gesture and mimicry from Garrick, whose acquaintance he made during several visits to England and with whom he eventually became very intimate. Admiration was mutual. Garrick dubbed his friend " the Shakespeare of the dance," and Noverre, at Voltaire's request, wrote two long letters in praise of Garrick and descriptive of his methods. Noverre, too, found a sympathetic co-adjutor in Gluck, who at that time was doing for opera what he himself was struggling to do for the ballet. They collaborated in the Ballet of the Savages in *Iphigénie in Tauris*. He was also associated with Mozart, who wrote the music for his ballet *Les petits Riens* (Paris, 1778); with Haydn at the King's Theatre, London (1791); with Piccinni, and at the close of his career with Cherubini.

It must not be imagined that Noverre succeeded in realising all, or anything like all, his ideas; the forces of reaction were too deeply entrenched. But he did succeed in impressing some of his theories upon his contemporaries and in initiating a reform which eventually freed the ballet from the traditional encumbrances which had barred its progress for the best part of the century.

The chief dancers contemporary with Noverre were Dauberval (1742-1806), his pupil and co-adjutor, Pierre Gardel (1758-1840), pupil of his brother Maximilien Gardel (1750-1787), and Gaetan Vestris (1729-1808), pupil of Dupré (who was taught by Beauchamps). In the opinion of Blasis, Dauberval and Pierre Gardel were the best choreographers of their day; their ballets being distinguished by an elegance and finish that were lacking in the works of Noverre. Gaetan Vestris succeeded Noverre and Gardel at Stuttgart. Vestris and Gardel introduced the *rond de jambe* into the ballet, and are said to have perfected the pirouette in the form known as the Grande Pirouette (à la seconde), *i.e.*, with the free leg held out horizontally to the side. Gaetan Vestris married Marie Allard (1742-1802), herself a distinguished dancer, and their son Auguste achieved as great a reputation as his father—who agreed that this was only natural, seeing that his son had this advantage over himself that he had Gaetan for a father. Auguste Vestris (Plate 56) was renowned for his high springs and cabrioles; indeed, so high and prolonged were they that Gaetan declared that if Auguste ever descended to earth it was out of consideration for the feelings of his less talented colleagues.

Of the women dancers of this period the best known were Larny, the first to execute the entrechat à six; Heinel, who, if she did not invent the pirouette, certainly aided its development; and Madeline Guimard (1753-1816), who danced in London from 1784-6.

By the end of the eighteenth century choreographers freed themselves from the limitations of the Court dances, and the dancers were no longer seriously hindered in the matter of dress or equipment. Masks had been given up since 1772 (Maximilien Gardel was the first to appear without one) and paniers, cuirasses and cumbersome head-dresses had disappeared. The shortening of the skirt and the occasional use of transparent material in its manufacture necessitated, however, a further evolution of the under-garment which Camargo was the first to wear, and this eventually resulted in the *maillot*, or skin-coloured tights. This invention is usually credited to Maillot, whose name it

44

FRANCE, XIX. CENTURY.

"CHAINE ANGLAISE." ILLUSTRATION TO THE ÉTRENNES À TERPSICHORE," A BOOK
OF CONTREDANSES. PARIS, c. 1820. COLOURED ENGRAVING.

PLATE 3.

bears. He was the costumier of the Paris opera at the beginning of the nineteenth century. There is, however, reason to believe that it, or something similar to it. was worn by Mlle. Guimard, who retired in 1790. After the Revolution La Rochefoucauld essayed to replace the maillot by the "grand pantalon," which enclosed both legs and extended well below the skirt; but this was short-lived, and pictures of Taglioni in *La Sylphide* (1832) show that by that time it had been discarded in favour of the maillot and the Greek tunic of gauze reaching below the knees. As the century advanced and greater technical demands were made upon the dancers, the skirt was gradually shortened till the limit was reached in the *tutu* which, together with the *maillot*, has since been universally adopted. These innovations were not, of course, effected without opposition, but the feeling in their favour was so strong that even the Pope found himself constrained to authorise the use of the *maillot* in the Papal Theatre—with the condition, however, that it should be dyed blue.

With the adoption of the short skirt and maillot and the disappearance of the Court dances the way was cleared for technical expansion, and so fully did dancers make use of their newly-won liberty that during the course of the nineteenth century the technique of the ballet was established upon an entirely new basis. So complete was this transformation that we may say without exaggeration that the ballet, as we know it to-day, is almost wholly the product of the nineteenth century. For this metamorphosis the Italians, and to a lesser extent the Russians, were mainly responsible, and early in the nineteenth century the centre of interest in theatrical dancing passed from Paris to Milan, with outposts at St. Petersburgh, Moscow and Warsaw.

The important figure at this critical moment in the history of the ballet was Carlo Blasis. He was a dancer (pupil of Gardel), composer. author of several works on dancing and kindred subjects, and a man of ability and education. He spent several years in England from 1826 onwards, and whilst in this country published (in English) the *Code of Terpsichore* (1830). His chief labours, however, were accomplished at Milan, first as dancer and maître de ballet at La Scala, afterwards, from 1837 onwards. as Director of the Imperial Academy of Dancing and Pantomime. Under his guidance the Milan Academy became the leading School in Europe, and through it he exercised a dominating influence upon the development of the ballet. The system of training which he instituted has since been imitated by all the important schools on the Continent. Students were not admitted to his Academy until after a year's probationary course in attitudes and a strict medical examination. The course lasted for eight years and included a daily practice, except on the prescribed holidays, of three hours' dancing in the morning and one hour's pantomime in the afternoon. That a course of such severity should have been considered necessary is proof of the high degree of technical proficiency which was demanded of the professional dancers of that day and of the importance which Blasis himself attached to the technical side of his art.

In the old days of long and heavily-weighted dresses the legs had of necessity played but a limited part in the dance, and dancers had depended for their effects upon the sway of the body and the gestures and movements of the arms. But now that the lower limbs were liberated, attention was concentrated upon the movements of the legs and, to judge by the retention of the tightly-laced bodice, with a consequent neglect of the torso, head and arms. This tendency was further emphasised by the discovery of the immense technical advantage that was to be gained by a certain modification of the positions of the feet in the " five positions."

Ever since Beauchamps first prescribed and taught them, the technique of dancing had been based upon the five fundamental positions of the feet, on one or other of which every step in the dance had to begin and end. These positions were first described in choreographic symbols by Feuillet (1701). They are given twenty-four years later, unaltered, in words as well as in pictures drawn by himself, by Rameau (*Maître à danser*, 1725) ; and again, still unchanged, by Malpied (*Traité sur l'art de la danse*, Paris, 1770 and 1780). In each of these treatises the feet were turned outward through an angle of 45 degrees. At Milan, however, under Blasis the students were required to turn them through an angle of 90 degrees, so that with heels joined the feet were in one line. It is difficult to fix precisely when this change took place, but it must have been between 1780, the year of Malpied's treatise—which must have been authoritative, since it was dedicated to Maximilien Gardel, then maître des ballets de l'Académie royale de musique—and 1820, when Blasis published his *Traité élémentaire*, in the diagrams of which the feet are fully turned out through an angle of 90 degrees. Solo-dancers may have adopted this position before 1780, but there is no evidence that they did so.

The technical advantage to be gained by turning out the feet had not escaped the notice of dancers in the previous century. A writer in the *Nécrologe des hommes célèbres de France* (1770) maintains that Camargo's dancing of minuets and passepieds was superior to that of Prévost's " parce que cette danseuse n'avait pas, comme elle, la pointe des pieds tournée en dehors, et par conséquent les hanches et les genoux " ; and Noverre, in one of his letters, advises students to turn out the feet in a similar way. The extreme, lateral, sole-position of the feet, which Blasis prescribed and which has since been universally adopted by ballet-dancers, though it has an awkward appearance through the unnatural outward flexion of the hip, knee and ankle-joints, has the great virtue that it provides the dancer with a wide base-line and a stance of great stability. It thus brings within his range a large number

46

Fig. (h)   Ballet positions from C. Blasis Traité Elémentaire (1820).

of difficult physical movements which he could not otherwise have attempted.   The dancer was not slow to perceive and to make the fullest use of his opportunity, and he soon learned to execute new varieties of entrechats, pirouettes, fouettés, extended leaps and other athletic feats, and to maintain himself in fresh and more difficult attitudes. But for this he was condemned to pay a heavy price.   He had to renounce once for all every normal, easy, natural method of motion— running, walking, slipping or skipping, and consequently to abandon all concerted figure movements.   I believe that it was this discovery which, more than any thing else, determined the evolution of the ballet in the nineteenth century and ultimately led it perilously near the border line—if indeed it did not at times actually overstep it—between the dance proper and the art, if it be one, of the gymnast or tumbler.

Toe-dancing is perhaps the most extreme instance of the virtuosity achieved by the ballet-dancers of the last century.   The position *sur la pointe* (Plate 68) is extremely difficult to acquire and one that needs long and painful practice before it can be used without danger of dislocating the upper joints of the toes. Even then it cannot be sustained without the artificial support of square, hard-toed slippers.   I cannot find that toe-dancing was practised at an earlier date than 1830.   Blasis, in his treatise of 1820, already quoted, constantly uses the expression *sur la pointe*, but from his diagrams (figure *h*) it is evident that by this he meant what is now known as the half-toe or *pied à trois quarts*—double proof that the point position as now understood was then unknown.   Noverre, who also used the expression, could only have given it the same sense.   If Taglioni was the first dancer to practise the modern position, as tradition credits her—and I cannot find any picture of an earlier dancer in this position—it did not come into vogue before 1830 (Plate 67).

It cannot be denied that at the end of the eighteenth century there was room for technical development nor that this has since been achieved. In the sureness, finish, accuracy and precision of their movements ballet-dancers have proved what may be effected when once complete mastery over the body and limbs has been attained. The value of this contribution cannot be over-estimated. Every artist, however, must, I think, deplore the uses to which this technical efficiency has been put. Wagner was certainly of this opinion and expressed it very trenchantly : " With her features cast in this unchangeable and fixed expression, she answers the demand for change and motion by her lower limbs alone : all her artistic capability has sunk down from her vertex through her body to her feet. Head, neck, trunk and thighs are only present as unbidden guests, whereas her feet have undertaken to show alone what she can do."

Already in the eighteenth century, when spectacular *tours de force* were comparatively few, Noverre was fully alive to the danger to which technical development might very easily lead, and he warned his contemporaries "that entrechats and cabrioles destroy all elegance in dancing," and added, "that as long as dancing is made to consist of tricks of strength and vaulting, an agreeable amusement will be turned into a debasing trade and dancing, far from progressing, will degenerate."

M. Svetlow is of opinion that the last years of the nineteenth century and the first years of the twentieth were those of the greatest decadence of the ballet. It was at this moment, at any rate, that a re-action set in and dancers from Moscow essayed the task of bringing about a reformation. Under the direction of M. Diaghilev they began a series of representations at the Théâtre du Châtelet in Paris in 1911. The principles by which they were guided were enunciated by M. Fokine at the time when the Russian dancers were appearing in London (*The Times*, July 6th, 1914). "The new ballet," he said, "rejects the conventions of the older ballet . . . with its artificial form of dancing on the point of the toe, with the feet turned out, dressed in short bodices, with the figure tightly laced in stays and with a strictly established system of steps, gestures and attitudes. If we look," he continued, " at the best productions of sculptural and pictorial art from the point of view of the choreographer of the old school thoroughly versed in the rules of traditional gesticulation and of dancing with the toes turned out, we shall find that the marble gods of Greece stood in entirely wrong attitudes. . . . If we are to be true to the rules of the older ballet we must turn our backs on the treasures of beauty accumulated by the genius of mankind during thousands of years and declare them all to be wrong."

How far M. Fokine and his colleagues have succeeded in translating their ideals into practice it is for those to judge who have followed

48

the remarkable series of ballets that they have presented in London and elsewhere in the last ten or fifteen years. There will, I am sure, be general agreement that they have placed the ballet on altogether a higher plane so far as scenery, costume, choice and character of subject, miming, stage-production and music are concerned. The dancing, however, is another matter; and here I cannot but think that they have been less successful. I have not noticed, for instance, that the Russian dancers have discontinued or found any substitutes for the virtuoso, acrobatic movements against which they rightly declaimed, the turned-out feet or "point" dancing. This was perhaps inevitable. M. Fokine and his co-adjutors were themselves trained in the technique, and saturated with the conventions, of the very type of dance that they essayed drastically to reform; and this, it seems, has proved a heavier handicap than they were able to carry. Nor, now that the ballet has become an exclusive, virtuoso art, is it easy to see how anyone who had not himself passed through the ballet schools would have the power to influence it.

A similar danger, it may be recalled, confronted the Florentine reformers of music three centuries ago. They were, however, fully sensible of the danger and guarded against it by refusing to admit to their councils any professional exponent of the music which they were trying to reform.

I am therefore of opinion—though I express it with some diffidence —that the better way to bring about the reform, and perhaps the line of least resistance is not to attempt an amendment of the existing ballet but to revert to first principles, to start afresh and endeavour to create a ballet founded upon one or other of our national folk-dance techniques. Many of the European nations could provide it. The technique of the English folk-dance, for example, is very full; it comprises a large number of different steps, arm and hand-movements and gestures and is especially rich in concerted figure-evolutions, a form of expression in the dance of which the ballet has hitherto made but little use. Here, surely, is sufficient material from which to develop a spectacular dance for the theatre which shall consist wholly of movements at once natural and expressive, and possessing the advantage for England that they are cast in the dance-idiom of our own country.

CECIL J. SHARP.

INDEX OF NAMES AND DANCES.

52

PLATE 4.

YOUTH AND DANCER. INTERIOR OF A RED-FIGURED CUP BY THE
"BRYGOS-PAINTER." *(British Museum, E.68).*

THE PYRRHIC DANCE. FROM THE MONUMENT ERECTED BY ATARBOS
TO CELEBRATE THE VICTORY OF HIS TEAM.
(Athens. Acropolis Museum).

RITUAL DANCE, PROBABLY AN ORPHIC CEREMONY. A STUCCO FROM
THE UNDERGROUND BASILICA NEAR THE PORTA MAGGIORE, ROME.
(Discovered in 1917.)

PLATE 5.

GRECO-ROMAN. 1st CENTURY B.C.

PLATE 6.

DANCING MAIDENS (perhaps a Spartan Dance). NEO-ATTIC RELIEF.
THREE HANDS RESTORED.   (Rome. Villa Albani).

DANCERS FROM A BOOK OF HOURS. FLEMISH. *c.* 1300.
(*British Museum. MS. Stowe, No.* 17).

PLATE 7.

ITALY. XIV. CENTURY.

PLATE 8. *AMBROGIO LORENZETTI.* DETAIL FROM THE FRESCO OF " GOOD
GOVERNMENT." 1337-39. *(Sienna. Palazzo Pubblico).*

PLATE 9.

A REVEL; DANCING (left) AND SINGING (right), WITH A MUMMERY AT THE
FOOT. A PAGE FROM THE ALEXANDER ROMANCE, A MANUSCRIPT OF
ABOUT 1340, IN THE BODLEIAN LIBRARY.

PLATE 10. "BRANLE DE LA SERVIETTE." MINIATURE FROM THE "ROMANCE OF RENAUD DE MONTAUBAN." (*Bibliothèque de l'Arsenal*).

ITALY. XV. CENTURY.

DANCING AND TUMBLERS. DETAIL FROM A MARRIAGE COFFER. FLORENTINE, c. 1475.
(In the Collection of the Rt. Honourable Viscount Lascelles).

PLATE 11.

ITALY. XV. CENTURY.

DANCE. DETAIL FROM A MARRIAGE COFFER. FLORENTINE SCHOOL, c. 1475.
(*In the Collection of the Rt. Honourable Viscount Lascelles*).

PLATE 12.

A CAROLE. FROM A MANUSCRIPT OF "THE ROMANCE OF THE ROSE."
(*British Museum, Harley MSS.* 4425).

PLATE 13.

GERMANY. XV. CENTURY.

PLATE 14.

ISRAHEL VAN MECKENEM. "THE RING DANCE." ENGRAVING.
(British Museum).

GERMANY. XV. CENTURY.

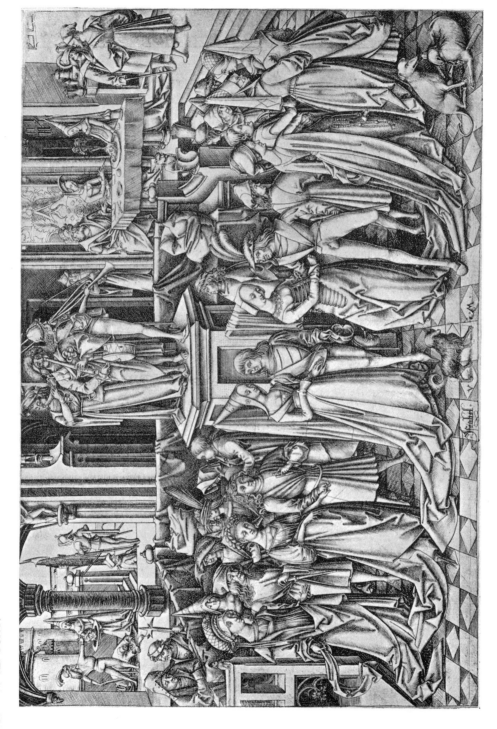

ISRAHEL VAN MECKENEM. "DANCE OF THE DAUGHTER OF HERODIAS." ENGRAVING.
(British Museum).

PLATE 15.

GERMANY. XV. CENTURY.

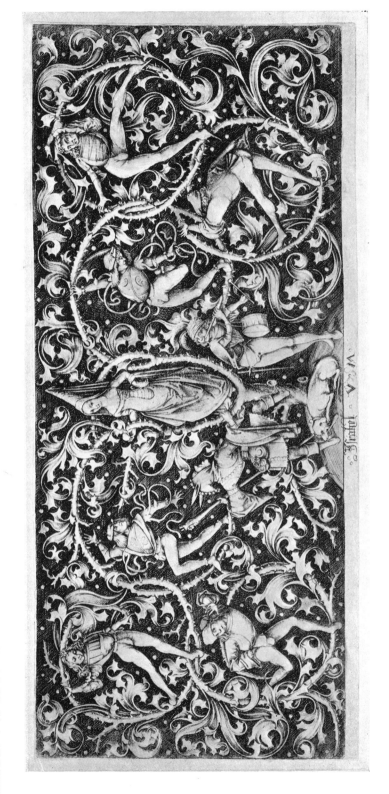

ISRAHEL VAN MECKENEM. ENGRAVED ORNAMENT WITH MEN DANCING.
(British Museum).

PLATE 16.

A. DURER or H. BURGKMAIR. MORISCO-DANCE. WOOD-CUT.
(British Museum).

PLATE 17.

GERMANY. XVI. CENTURY.

SWORD DANCE OF THE CUTLERS' GUILD. PEN DRAWING.
(Nuremburg. Germanisches Museum).

NETHERLANDS. XVI. CENTURY.

EARLY DUTCH SCHOOL. AN OPEN-AIR DANCE. PEN DRAWING.
(New York. Metropolitan Museum).

PLATE 18.

FLANDERS OR GERMANY. XVI. CENTURY.

THEODOR DE BRY. COURT DANCE (perhaps the Pavane) AND A RUSTIC DANCE.
ENGRAVING.
(*British Museum*).

PLATE 19.

PLATE 20.

FRENCH SCHOOL. A VILLAGE DANCE. OIL PAINTING
(Montpellier. *Musée Fabre*).

NETHERLANDS. XVi CENTURY.

PIETER AERTSZ. THE EGG-DANCE. 1557. OIL PAINTING.
(Amsterdam. Rijks Museum).

PLATE 21.

GERMAN EMPIRE. XVI. CENTURY.

PLATE 22.

MONOGRAMMATIST "F.A." 1560. BALL AT THE EMPEROR'S PALACE, VIENNA.
(British Museum).
ENGRAVING.

NETHERLANDS. XVI. CENTURY.

PETER BREUGHEL. "THE KERMESSE OF ST. GEORGE." c. 1560. ENGRAVING.
(British Museum).

PLATE 23.

ENGLAND. XVI. CENTURY.

IORIS HOEFNAGEL. "A WEDDING AT HORSLEYDOWN, NEAR SOUTHWARK." c. 1569.
OIL PAINTING. (In the Collection of the Rt. Hon. The Marquis of Salisbury).

PLATE 24.

FRONTISPIECE TO THE "BALLET COMIQUE DE LA
REINE" OF BALTAZARINI, called BEAUJOYEULX. 1582.
(British Museum).

PLATE 25.

FRANCE OR FLANDERS. XVI. CENTURY.

FLEMISH SCHOOL. *perhaps HIERONYMUS FRANCKEN.* A COURT BALL. OIL PAINTING.
(*Carlsruhe*).

PLATE 26.

FRANCE. XVI. CENTURY.

HERMAN VAN DER MAST. A BALL AT THE COURT OF HENRI III. c. 1575. OIL PAINTING.
(Paris. Louvre).

PLATE 27.

PLATE 28.

GIULIO PARIGI—J. CALLOT. FIRST SCENE OF THE GRAND BALLET AT
FLORENCE IN 1616. "THE GIANT TYPHOEUS BELOW MOUNT ISCHIA."
ETCHING.   (British Museum).

FRANCE. XVII. CENTURY.

BALLET DANSÉ PAR LE ROI, " LA DÉLIVRANCE DE PERSÉE." Jan. 29th, 1617. ENGRAVINGS.
(*British Museum*).

PLATE 29.

ENGLAND. XVII. CENTURY.

FLEMISH SCHOOL. MORRIS DANCE NEAR SHEEN PALACE. OIL PAINTING.
(Cambridge. *Fitzwilliam Museum*).

PLATE 30.

I. *CALLOT* or *STEFANO DELLA BELLA*. DESIGN FOR A FAN. UNFINISHED
ETCHING.   (*British Museum*).

PLATE 31.

"BALLET DES RIDICULES." 1628. No. 15, "ENTRÉE DES DEMI-FOUX."
WATER-COLOUR. *(Paris. Bibliothèque Nationale).*

"BALLET DES QUATRE PARTIES DU MONDE." 1629. No. 26, "SARABAND
DANCERS." WATER-COLOUR. *(Paris. Bibliothèque Nationale).*

PLATE 32.

PLATE 33.

INIGO JONES.   SKETCHES FOR FIGURES IN THE ANTIMASQUE
" BRITANNIA TRIUMPHANS."   1637.
(In the Collection of the Duke of Devonshire)

PLATE 34.

INIGO JONES. CHARACTERS IN AN ANTIMASQUE. *c.* 1635. BRUSH
DRAWING. *(In the Collection of the Duke of Devonshire).*

ITALY. XVII. CENTURY.

QARTA SCENA DI MARE

ALFONSO PARIGI—STEFANO DELLA BELLA. SCENE IV. FROM THE "NOZZE DEGLI DEI"
PERFORMED AT FLORENCE FOR THE MARRIAGE OF DUKE FERDINAND II. AND VITTORIA
OF URBINO. 1637. ENGRAVING.
(British Museum).

PLATE 35.

ITALY. XVII. CENTURY.

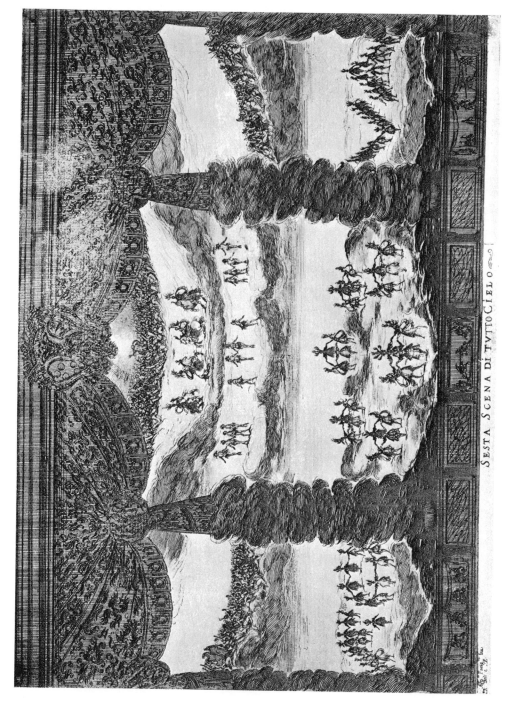

SESTA SCENA DI TVTTO CIELO

ALFONSO PARIGI—STEFANO DELLA BELLA. SCENE VI. FROM THE "NOZZE DEGLI DEI"
PERFORMED AT FLORENCE. 1637. ENGRAVING.
(British Museum).

PLATE 36.

ITALY. XVII. CENTURY.

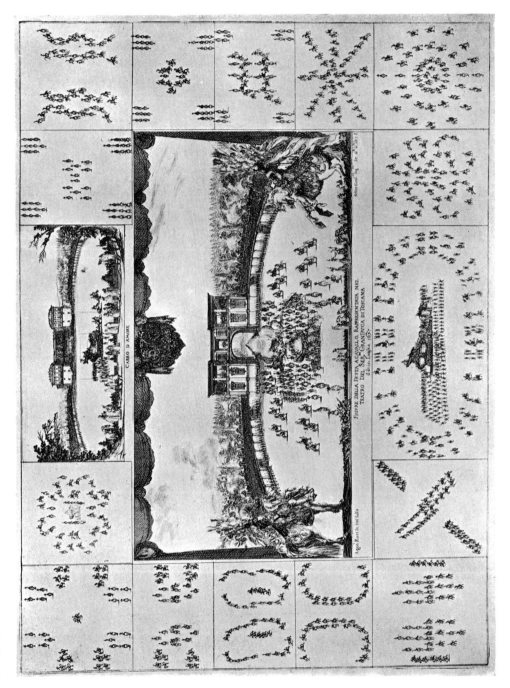

STEFANO DELLA BELLA. HORSE BALLET AT FLORENCE. 1637. ENGRAVING.
(British Museum).

PLATE 37.

NETHERLANDS. XVII. CENTURY.

P. P. RUBENS. "THE VILLAGE DANCE." OIL PAINTING.
(Madrid. Prado).

Plate 38.

PLATE 39.

P. P. RUBENS. STUDIES FOR THE "VILLAGE FESTIVAL" IN THE
LOUVRE. PEN DRAWING.   (*British Museum*).

HOLLAND. XVII. CENTURY.

HIERONYMUS JANSSENS (1624-1693). KING CHARLES II. DANCING AT A BALL AT THE
HAGUE. (A CORANTO). OIL PAINTING AT WINDSOR CASTLE.
(*Copyright of H.M. The King*).

PLATE 40.

PLATE 41.

D. MAROT. THE GREAT BALL AT THE HAGUE ON THE BIRTHDAY OF
THE PRINCE OF ORANGE. 1686. ENGRAVING. *(British Museum).*

PLATE 42.

A. WATTEAU. "FETE CHAMPETRE." (A MINUET). OIL PAINTING.
(Edinburgh. National Gallery of Scotland).

FRANCE. XVIII. CENTURY.

N. LANCRET. MADEMOISELLE CAMARGO. c. 1730. OIL PAINTING.
(London. Hertford House).

PLATE 43.

ENGLAND. XVIII. CENTURY.

PLATE 44.

A. VANHAECKEN. THE MINUET: THE CONCLUSION, OR PRESENTING BOTH ARMS. ILLUSTRATION TO KELLON TOMLINSON'S "ART OF DANCING." 1735. (*Victoria and Albert Museum*).

AUSTRIA. XVIII. CENTURY.

GIUSEPPE BIBBIENA—J. A. PFEFFEL. BALL IN THE IMPERIAL STABLES, VIENNA, FOR
THE BETROTHAL OF THE GRAND DUCHESS MARIANNA AND CHARLES OF LORRAINE. 1744.
(British Museum).

PLATE 45.

PLATE 46.   G. *SCOTIN*. MADEMOISELLE AURETTI. ENGRAVING.

W. HOGARTH. "THE COUNTRY DANCE," or "THE HAPPY MARRIAGE." 1753. ENGRAVING.

PLATE 47.

AUSTRIA. XVIII. CENTURY.

PLATE 48. B. BELLOTTO. BALLET PANTOMIME. "LE TURC GÉNÉREUX." VIENNA, 26th April, 1758.
ENGRAVING.

THE BALLET "PYGMALION" DANCED AT AMSTERDAM, 1758, BY THE
SISTERS FREDERIC, AGED 9 AND 7 YEARS. ENGRAVING AFTER G. VAN
DER MYN, BY J. PUNT. (*Mr. F. R. Meatyard*).

PLATE 49.

FRANCE. XVIII. CENTURY.

PLATE 50.

G. DE ST. AUBIN. "LE BAL D'AUTEUIL." FRONTISPIECE TO THE
"REPERTOIRE DE BALS" OF LA CUISSE. 1761. ETCHING.

(Victoria and Albert Museum).

FRANCE. XVIII. CENTURY.

GABRIEL DE ST. AUBIN. "BALLET DES FEES." FROM THE SKETCH-BOOK. "SCENES
THEATRALES."
(Private Collection).

PLATE 51.

FRANCE. XVIII. CENTURY.

S. A. SLODTZ. "LE BAL DU MAI." DANCED AT VERSAILLES AT THE CARNIVAL OF 1763. WATER-COLOUR.
(In the Collection of His Excellency, the Hon. Irwin Laughlin, Washington).

PLATE 52.

ENGLAND. XVIII. CENTURY.

J. COLLET—J. CALDWELL. THE COTILLON DANCE. 1771. ENGRAVING.

PLATE 53.

ENGLAND. XVIII. CENTURY.

C. BRANDOIN—J. CALDWELL. THE ALLEMANDE DANCE. 1772. ENGRAVING. (British Museum).

PLATE 54

FRANCE. XVIII. CENTURY.

Le Bal
A Monsieur de

Pare
Villemorien Fils

A. DE ST. AUBIN—A. I. DUCLOS. "LE BAL PARÉ." c. 1773. ENGRAVING.
(British Museum).

PLATE 55.

PLATE 56.

NATHANIEL DANCE, R.A. "THE STRANGER AT SPARTA" (VESTRIS).
1780. ETCHING. (British Museum).

NATHANIEL DANCE, R.A. BALLET OF JASON AND MEDEA. 1781. AQUATINT.
(British Museum).

PLATE 57.

H. W. BUNBURY. "THE DANCERS." COLOURED CHALK DRAWING. (ENGRAVED 1782 BY BARTOLOZZI). (*Mr. Frank T. Sabin*).

PLATE 58

T. GAINSBOROUGH, R.A. "MADAME BACCELLI." MEZZOTINT BY T.
JONES. 1784. FIRST PUBLISHED STATE.   *(Mr. Frank T. Sabin).*

PLATE 59.

ENGLAND. XVIII. CENTURY.

T. ROWLANDSON. A HORNPIPE AND A LONGWAYS DANCE (1790). ETCHINGS.

PLATE 60.

ENGLAND. XVIII. CENTURY.

H. W. BUNBURY—W. DICKINSON. THE LONG MINUET AS DANCED AT BATH. 1794.
COLOURED AQUATINT. (Mr. W. T. Spencer).

PLATES 61 AND 62.

FRANCE. XIX. CENTURY.

FRANCE. XIX. CENTURY.

B. ZIX—C. QUERIN. A BALL AT THE COURT OF NAPOLEON. c. 1810. ENGRAVING.

PLATE 64.

ENGLAND. XIX. CENTURY.

THE WALTZ. THE REFERENCE PLATE TO WILSON'S " DESCRIPTION OF GERMAN AND FRENCH WALTZING." 1816.

PLATE 65.

FRANCE. XIX. CENTURY.

GAVARNI. "UN BAL À LA CHAUSSÉE D'ANTIN. 1830. LITHOGRAPH.
(*British Museum*).

PLATE 66.

A. E. CHALON. MLLE. TAGLIONI. 1831. LITHOGRAPH BY R. J. LANE.

PLATE 67.

PLATE 68.

J. BOUVIER. LOUISE FLEURY. PAS DE DIANE IN THE BALLET, "THE BEAUTY OF GHENT." *c.* 1840. COLOURED LITHOGRAPH

(*Mr. W. T. Spencer*).

C. *VERNIER*. LA POLKA. COLOURED LITHOGRAPH.

PLATE 69.

FRANCE. XIX. CENTURY.

E. LAMI. "BAL MASQUÉ A L'OPÉRA." STEEL ENGRAVING.
(British Museum)

PLATE 70.

Photo. A. Giraudon

E. DEGAS. "REPÉTITION D'UN BALLET." OIL PAINTING.
(*Paris. Louvre*).

PLATE 71.

Photo. A. Giraudon

PLATE 72.

E. DEGAS. "DANSEUSE SUR LA SCÈNE." PASTEL.
(Paris. Luxembourg).

JOHN COPLEY. " PAVLOVA." LITHOGRAPH.
(P. & D. Colnaghi & Co.).

PLATE 73.

PLATE 74.

LAURA KNIGHT. " LES SYLPHIDES." OIL PAINTING.
(In the Collection of Major P. C. Bull, D.S.O.).

C. R. W. NEVINSON. "THE DANCER." OIL PAINTING.
(In the Collection of Mrs. R. J. Symonds).

PLATE 75.